A GOOD DAY FOR

SALAD

A GOOD DAY FOR SALAD

by Louise Fiszer and Jeannette Ferrary

CHRONICLE
BOOKS

Library of Congress Cataloging-in-Publication Data:

Fiszer, Louise.
  A good day for salad/by Louise Fiszer and Jeannette Ferrary.
    p.   cm.
  ISBN 0-8118-1991-4 (pbk.)
1. Salads. I. Ferrary, Jeannette   II. Title
641.8'3—dc21
                          99-19497
                          CIP

Printed in the United States of America.

Designed by Patricia Evangelista
Photographed by Dwight Eschliman
Prop and food styling by Darrell Coughlan
Illustrated by A DOZEN MOTHS

Distributed in Canada by Raincoast Books
8680 Cambie Street
Vancouver, British Columbia V6P 6M9

10 9 8 7 6 5 4 3 2 1

Chronicle Books
85 Second Street
San Francisco, California 94105

www.chroniclebooks.com

DEDICATION

For Natasha, as she begins making her own salads
and everything else for that matter, with all my
love—JF

For my Max, Michael, and Mitchell, who make
life a joyous and well-seasoned salad toss—LF

CONTENTS

INTRODUCTION

"GRASS IS FOR COWS!"

Uncle Boris always grumbled as he pushed the bowl of greens to the side of his dinner plate. And even after Aunt Mildred reminded him, very quietly, that "salad is good for you, dear," he would fork up a few leaves with reluctance. In a way, maybe Uncle Boris had a point about what passed for salad back then, but in the past few years salads have changed dramatically. They've expanded from the ubiquitous daily chunk of iceberg to an assortment of greens with tastes of their own: bitter, tangy, sweet, minty, spicy, peppery. They have broadened their scope of ingredients to include chopped vegetables, rice and legumes, seafood, grains, meats, every kind of pasta. These days, ironically, it is not unusual to find salads that contain no greens at all.

A glance at today's restaurant menus tells the story. They include salads, usually quite a few of them. But many of the other dishes throughout the menu are also essentially salads, although they may be called everything from side dishes, vegetable entrées, and first courses to sandwiches, cold pastas, and main dishes. Quite often, it is the salad dishes (by whatever name) that tantalize you with their little creative flourishes, their sparkle, the intriguing contrasts that make them irresistible. Today's chefs obviously enjoy playing with the panorama of textures and tastes, color and fragrance that salads allow them to assemble.

For the home cook, who usually does not have a massive array of ingredients immediately at hand, things have to be a little more organized. In *A Good Day for Salad,* we have tried to capture the sparkle and excitement of contemporary salads in a practical, helpful format tailored to today's lifestyles. In this approach, we show how salad can be the answer to just about any of the staggering number of mealtime scenarios that confront today's home cook. Salad can be the solution to almost any meal occasion: it can be any course in a family meal, or it can be the life of a fancy party; it can be made quickly from pantry-ready ingredients, or it can be a warm and cozy comfort food; it is always the perfect meal in summer and spring and, with gutsy, stick-to-the-ribs ingredients like lentils, sausages, and grains, it makes fantastic meals for fall and winter; and best of all, it can be totally cooked, totally cook-less, and everything in between.

A Good Day for Salad tells the history of salad through its myriad incarnations and shows how each generation creates salads appropriate to its own times. We introduce each recipe with information and headnotes that, we hope, are both helpful and enjoyable to read. We've tried to make *A Good Day for Salad* comprehensive, lively, and fun. Maybe it's too much to hope for, but we think there may even be a thing or two to please the likes of Uncle Boris.

THE HISTORY OF SALAD:
A SHORT COURSE ON THE FIRST COURSE

According to historians of early America, when the first Europeans came to this fresh and fertile land, they were overwhelmed by the goodness and variety of the vegetation. In fact, while they waited for their chunks of meat to cook over open fires, they could never resist nibbling away at the nearest greenery. Presumably, these wilderness habits were eventually refined into an attraction to salads.

HOWEVER, the difficulties of farming on the American frontier encouraged the planting of only the hardiest of root vegetables, potatoes, cabbages, and pumpkins. Farm people subsisted on corn bread, pork, and salted fish, with few, if any, vegetables. Eating raw foods had its hazards, not only because of unhygienic handling and storage, but also because certain epidemics ran rampant in summer when fresh vegetables were in season. Although this association was more coincidental than causative, it reinforced a fear of uncooked produce. "Beware of saladis," prescribed the ancient wisdom in John Russell's *Boke of Nurture* (1460), "and of fruites rawe."

IN THE 1800S, tomatoes were rare and considered dangerous. Cookbooks advised boiling vegetables to oblivion, dropping sliced cucumbers immediately into cold water, and throwing away the water that potatoes were cooked in. Isabella Beeton's *Book of Household Management* (1861) warned that radishes "are the cause of headaches when eaten to excess." Many cookbooks made no mention of salads at all. Menus for state occasions of the period list a plethora of dishes but consistently omit a salad course.

PEOPLE IN this country were also suspicious of olive oil, which was frequently laced with cheaper, often rancid oils. Vinegars, adulterated with all manner of insalubrious acids, were always suspect. Boiled dressings and bottled condiments were the common solution. People did eat composed salads, however, made with assorted cooked ingredients. German Americans turned potato salad into an American institution. The Dutch contributed coleslaw to the sweet-sour category of salads, and soul-food cooks made "hog maw" from celery and peppers, with results that hinted at chicken salad. Scandinavians offered their cold tables and the traditions of the Swedish smorgasbord; pre-meal munching gained popularity with the arrival of Italians and their antipasto. But only the upper classes had green, leafy salads, or even wanted them.

IN FACT, salads were so associated with the wealthy that cooks were not permitted to make the salad course: "I never allow a servant even to touch the leaves of the salad I have served at table," wrote Mrs. Bayard Taylor in *Letters of a Young Housekeeper* (1892), "for to have the salad to perfection the touch must be light, the fingers to trim and arrange be nimble." New York's Delmonico's restaurant, which opened in 1831, pioneered the creation of salads for its wealthy clientele using New World ingredients. Still, the average American at that time, according to Richard Hooker's *History of Food and Drink in America,* "probably did not eat salads at all."

AROUND the turn of the century, as people moved to the cities, which meant more sedentary living, they became interested in less substantial meals. Slowly but surely, salads started to become, in Hooker's words, the "plaything of the adventurous." Fannie Farmer's 1906 cookbook advised that salads could be made from "watercress, chicory, cucumbers, etc.," which contain "little nutriment, but are cooling."

Her recipe for East India Salad, which begins "Work two ten cent cream cheeses until smooth," indicates an experimental spirit that can also be seen in such popular concoctions as Porcupine Salad—a pear stuck with almond slivers—and Golf Salad—a mixture of hard-cooked egg yolks and mayonnaise rolled into balls covered with cottage cheese. The Drum Major Salad was constructed of tomato slices to form the "drum," while stuffed olives fitted to carrot sticks became the drumsticks. The ultimate in contrivances was the jellied vegetable mishmash called Perfection Salad, the brainchild of Mrs. John Cooke, who entered it in a salad competition sponsored by the Knox Gelatin people in 1905. Among the judges was Fannie Farmer herself. Maximilian De Loup, the foresightful author of the *American Salad Book,* predicted in 1900 that Americans would some day accept salads and even prefer them over "heavy bulky materials." He exhorted his countrymen to be proud of the variety and abundance of vegetables and not to feel intimidated by the less bountifully endowed French or by the English, whom he called "still barbaric" in their dealings with salads. In the 1920s, the fascinating *Edgewater Beach Hotel Salad Book* announced that the salad, as a culinary form, had reached perfection in America. It further declared that "American women have made the salad an American institution."

MEANWHILE, back at the gold mines, Californians by contrast had early recognized that the value of salads could be monetary as well as nutritional. Those who pioneered in produce realized considerable profits from the cultivation and marketing of "green gold." This early exposure probably explains why Californians have always been more experimental about salads than just about anybody outside the Mediterranean. "To my knowledge, California is the only place where truck drivers eat fresh salads without fear of being considered effete," says Jonathan Leonard in *American Cooking: The Great West.* San Diego patrons reportedly beat a path to the door of Caesar Cardini's Tijuana restaurant when he created the now-famous Caesar salad. The credit for crab Louis is in dispute, but San Francisco's St. Francis Hotel and the old Solari restaurant have the most plausible claims to authorship. The Palace Hotel in San Francisco celebrated the presence of George Arliss, touring in the play *The Green Goddess,* by creating an appropriately named salad dressing in his honor. Traveling west to California one hundred years ago, a visitor asserted that the avocado and shrimp salads of San Francisco "made the trip worthwhile" and dubbed California the "land of salads."

THESE DAYS, this nickname might be used for the whole country, especially with the rise of farmers' markets and vegetable gardening, even in urban areas. This contagious interest in and availability of salad "makin's" means that the salad is now often the center of the meal and its most colorful course.

ADDRESSING THE SALAD

DRESSED TO THRILL: OILS AND VINEGARS

Olive Oil

FRUITY, peppery, lush, grassy, robust, herbaceous, sweet, assertive, earthy—these words describe the desirable effects of olive oil. Not surprisingly, the finer the oil, the more profoundly you'll experience these pleasurable qualities. All olive oils begin with the crushing of the olives followed by an analysis of the resulting liquid. The lower the percentage of oleic acid, which accelerates oxidation and spoilage, the better the oil. Extra-virgin olive oil can contain no more than 1 percent acid, superfine $1\frac{1}{2}$ percent, fine 3 percent, and virgin up to 4 percent. Labels of extra-virgin oils will contain the words *first cold pressing,* meaning that no heat or chemical processes were used to extract the oil. Some producers also list acid content, vintage, the kinds of olives used, and notes about the harvest.

AFTER the first cold pressing, subsequent pressings, filters, chemicals, and additives are used to extract more oil, lower the acid content, remove off- flavors and colors, and otherwise refine the resulting liquid. Pure olive oil is a mixture of refined oils plus a dollop of extra-virgin oil for taste. Although these lesser oils may be fine for cooking, cold-pressed extra-virgin olive oil, with its voluptuous aroma and color and rich olive taste, is unquestionably the preferred choice for bringing out the best in most salads. Because extra-virgin tastes of the country, region, and conditions of its origin, it's a good idea to keep several brands on hand for matching with your ingredients.

A WORD ABOUT COLOR: Olive oils range from deep, earthy green to sunny yellow. Color may indicate the ripeness of the olives, but it is no determinant of quality.

STORE olive oil in a cool place away from light and heat. Tinted bottles provide extra protection. Do not refrigerate, which can cause condensation and rancidity. Use within a year or two.

Other Oils

WALNUT, hazelnut, almond, and other nut oils can make delicious dressings, as can seed oils like sesame and grapeseed oil.

THERE are many types of vinegars, some of which, such as seasoned rice vinegar and balsamic vinegar, are flavorful enough to serve as dressings on their own. Herb-flavored vinegars, such as tarragon white wine vinegar, add their own character to a plain salad, while fruit-steeped vinegars, such as raspberry or currant vinegar, are especially good with fruit or vegetable salads. But the basis of most salad dressings is a good wine vinegar, what the French call *vinaigre,* or "sour wine."

WINE VINEGAR, white or red, is essentially grape juice left to oxidize slowly, thus forming the bacteria that turns the wine to vinegar. The best-quality wine vinegars are aged in wooden barrels to develop and mature their flavors and aromas. As with wine, the color comes from the grape skins left in the juice before it is strained. Wine vinegars may be identified by the grape variety or wine they are made from, such as Zinfandel, sherry, or Champagne.

Balsamic Vinegar

A STORE with a well-stocked section of balsamic vinegars provides a lot of confusion. Prices can range from a few dollars to a few hundred dollars for a tiny, though intriguing-looking, bottle. Actually, price is an excellent clue to the mysteries of balsamic quality, assuming the store is a reputable one.

BROADLY SPEAKING, there are two types of balsamic vinegars: traditional—or *tradizionale*—and industrial. In Modena, Italy, the ancestral home of balsamic vinegar, every aspect of the production of traditional balsamic is strictly regulated, from the growing of the sweet Trebbiano grapes to the shape of the bottle. After harvest, grapes are crushed and the resulting must "cooked," or boiled down to concentrate the sugars. The must is then filtered, allowed to ferment slowly, and finally aged in wooden barrels. Vinegars aged twenty-five years or longer, called *extra vecchio,* command the highest prices. A good-quality balsamic vinegar has a deep, rich, complex taste, with a delicate balance of acid and sweetness. A few drops stirred into some excellent olive oil make a sublime dressing.

INDUSTRIAL balsamic vinegars, the kind available in most supermarkets, avoid the costly aging process and use herbs, spices, and sometimes less-appetizing additives to simulate the complex aromas and flavors of the real thing. In recipes where the vinegar is used in quantity or mixed with other ingredients, industrial balsamics are an acceptable and more affordable alternative.

Raspberry Vinegar

CALIFORNIA produces excellent raspberry vinegars, usually from a mix of white wine vinegar and crushed fresh raspberries. Like the fruit itself, raspberry vinegar should have an acid edge and a subtle, not cloying, sweetness.

Sherry Vinegar

THE BEST sherry vinegars come from Spain and are aged in wood barrels for as long as twenty years. Their nutty flavor marries well with olive oil and with all nut oils. Sherry vinegar adds interest to a freshly made mayonnaise destined to top a fish or seafood salad.

GREENS WITH ENVY:
A GUIDE TO SEASONAL GREENS

THE *Boston Cooking-School Cook Book* of 1906, by Fannie Merritt Farmer, rejoiced that salads, which "but a few years since seldom appeared on the table," were "now made in an endless variety of ways." Fannie herself would probably be amazed at the sheer number of our current choices.

LOOK for seasonal greens with sparkling fresh leaves without bruising or wilting. Store salad greens, unwashed, loosely wrapped in paper towels and then in plastic bags or wrap, and refrigerate for up to 5 days. As needed, thoroughly wash and dry all greens including, for utmost safety, greens that come prewashed and dried. If desired, washed and dried greens can be rolled in toweling and crisped in refrigerator for several hours before being dressed just before serving. According to Harold McGee's evidence in *The Curious Cook,* there is no basis for the adage that tearing greens is superior to cutting them with a knife.

SOME of the more popular greens, along with their aliases and more salient characteristics, include:

ARUGULA, ALSO CALLED ROCKET, RUGULA, ROQUETTE, OR ROCKET CRESS: An unmistakable relative of the cabbage with a pungent, slightly peppery, nutty, and sometimes bitter taste.

BELGIAN ENDIVE: Ivory colored, delicately bitter, crisp.

BIBB, OR LIMESTONE, LETTUCE: Crispy leaves, small heads.

BUTTER, OR BOSTON, LETTUCE: Loose-leafed; delicate taste and texture.

CHICORY, CURLY FRISÉE, OR CURLY ENDIVE: Green, feathery leaves; slightly bitter.

DANDELION GREENS: Tangy, flavorful leaves.

ESCAROLE: Heavier than chicory, with less frilly leaves, wide ribs, and a tougher texture but a tender heart.

ICEBERG LETTUCE: An all-purpose, bland-tasting lettuce that goes in and out of fashion but is unbeaten for its combination of sturdiness, year-round availability, and crunch.

LEAF LETTUCE, RED-LEAF LETTUCE, GARDEN LETTUCE: Tender, curly, delicate leaves that wilt quickly.

MÂCHE, ALSO CALLED CORN SALAD, LAMB'S LETTUCE, OR FIELD LETTUCE: A tangy dark-green rosette of leaves with a mild but stimulating flavor; delicious with cooked beets.

MESCLUN: A mix of greens that provide a bouquet of flavors, textures, tastes, and levels of crunch.

MIZUNA: A member of the Asian mustard family; silver and green leaves add texture and delicate flavor.

ORACH: Delicate, sweet, tender leaves ranging in color from red and green to yellow.

RADICCHIO: A magenta-colored, bitter-leafed type of chicory; round Verona, tapered Treviso, and crinkly, white-striped Chiogga are most common.

ROMAINE: Crunchy midribs and dark green elongated leaves; famous in Caesar salad.

SALAD BURNET: Has the smell and taste of cucumber; once revered as a privileged member of Napoleon's daily salad, often paired with wild chicory (though he preferred dried haricot beans).

WATERCRESS: Dark green, mildly peppery, refreshing.

THESE are only a few of the possibilities; there are also red and green chards, several sorrels, spinach, various other cresses. Farmers'-market mixes are increasingly popular for their exciting, palate-provoking tastes and textures but mainly for their unpredictability: They may include red mustards, baby spinaches, pea shoots, red romaines, and anything else the farmer chooses to grow. Salad mixes from the supermarket are also gaining in favor for their ease of use and variety. These usually organic mixes of whatever is in season make salad-tossing a breeze.

SALAD SPRINKLINGS

These little scatterings provide that final touch of taste, texture, and color that can elevate a simple bowl of greens into a sparkling taste sensation. Other possibilities include a handful of crumbled bacon, a snowfall of feta, slivers of tasty Parmigiano-Reggiano.

CRISPY CAPERS

Sprinkle on fish salads.

2 tablespoons olive oil
$1/4$ cup capers, drained and rinsed

IN A MEDIUM SKILLET over medium heat, heat oil until hot. Blot excess moisture from capers with paper towels and add to hot oil. Cook until capers pop and turn a dark green. Using a slotted spoon, transfer to paper towels to drain.

FRIED CELERY LEAVES

Sprinkle on chicken and seafood salads.

3 tablespoons vegetable oil
1 cup celery leaves
Salt and freshly ground pepper to taste

IN A MEDIUM SKILLET over medium heat, heat oil until hot. Add celery leaves and fry until crisp and golden, about 2 minutes. Using a slotted spoon, transfer to paper towels to drain. Sprinkle with salt and pepper.

GARLIC CROUTONS

Use in Caesar or other green salads.

2 tablespoons butter
2 tablespoons olive oil
2 cloves garlic, minced
6 slices firm white bread or French bread,
   cut into ½-inch cubes

PREHEAT OVEN to 350°F. In a large skillet, melt butter with oil and garlic over medium heat. Add bread cubes and stir until all are coated with oil mixture. Transfer to a baking sheet and spread in a single layer. Bake until lightly browned and crisp, about 20 minutes. Let cool.

BAKED GOAT CHEESE ROUNDS

Serve warm on a bed of dressed salad greens.

One 6-ounce log fresh white goat cheese
6 tablespoons extra-virgin olive oil
¹/₃ cup dried bread crumbs
¹/₂ teaspoon dried thyme
¹/₂ teaspoon dried oregano

SLICE GOAT CHEESE into ¹/₂-inch-thick rounds. Mix bread crumbs with herbs and spread on a sheet of waxed paper. Pour 4 tablespoons oil into a shallow bowl. Dip goat cheese into oil to coat completely, then into bread crumb mixture. Set on a tray and refrigerate for 1 hour. **PREHEAT OVEN** to 375°F. Spread remaining 2 tablespoons olive oil on a baking sheet with sides. Place goat cheese rounds on baking sheet and bake until a golden crust forms, about 8 minutes. Turn rounds over and bake another 3 minutes.

SWEET AND PEPPERY NUTS

Sprinkle on salads of greens and fruit, or greens and pungent cheeses such as Roquefort.

1/4 cup sugar

2 cups (8 ounces) coarsley chopped walnuts,
    pecans, peanuts, or almonds

1 teaspoon ground pepper or to taste

IN A LARGE nonstick skillet, heat sugar over medium heat until it begins to look moist. Add nuts and stir until nuts are hot and appear shiny and glazed. Sprinkle with pepper and turn out on a piece of waxed paper to cool.

FRIZZLED LEEKS

Sprinkle on delicate greens and tomato salads.

Vegetable or canola oil for deep-frying
4 leeks, white part only, washed and thinly sliced
Salt and freshly ground pepper to taste

IN A SMALL, heavy saucepan, heat about 2 inches of oil to 350°F. Add leeks and fry until golden brown and frizzled. Using a slotted spoon, transfer to paper towels to drain. Sprinkle with salt and pepper.

CRISPY WONTON RIBBONS

Sprinkle on Asian-style salads.

Peanut oil for frying
1 package wonton skins, cut into ½-inch strips
½ teaspoon ground coriander
½ teaspoon ground cumin
Salt and freshly ground pepper to taste

IN A HEAVY, medium saucepan, heat oil to 350°F. Drop about 5 or 6 wonton strips into hot oil and cook until curled and golden. Using a slotted spoon, transfer to paper towels to drain. Repeat to cook remaining strips. Sprinkle with coriander, cumin, salt, and pepper.

GARLIC CROSTINI

Twelve ³/₄-inch-thick slices country-style bread
Olive oil for brushing
1 clove garlic, halved

PREHEAT OVEN to 375°F. Lightly brush both sides of bread with oil. Place on a baking sheet and toast until golden brown, about 8 minutes per side. While still warm, rub each side of crostini with a cut clove of garlic. Spread with a favorite topping.

TOASTING COCONUT, SEEDS, AND NUTS

IN A LARGE, dry, nonstick skillet, cook coconut, seeds, or nuts over medium heat until they become fragrant and take on color, shaking pan frequently. Seeds and coconut take about 3 minutes, nuts about 5 minutes.

ROASTING AND PEELING PEPPERS

ROAST PEPPERS on a baking sheet in a preheated 450°F oven until charred and blistered. Transfer peppers to a paper bag, close, and let cool. Rub off blistered skin and remove seeds and ribs.

PEELING AND SECTIONING CITRUS FRUITS

WITH A LARGE SHARP KNIFE, cut a slice from top and bottom of fruit down to the flesh. Stand fruit upright on one end. (If juice from fruit is to be used, do this over a bowl.) Cut down fruit to remove peel down to the flesh and remove as much pith as possible without cutting into the flesh. To section, cut in between membranes to release segments.

VARIATIONS ON A VINAIGRETTE

The following are simple, straightforward dressings for a variety of salads.

BASIC VINAIGRETTE

3 tablespoons red or white wine vinegar
   or fresh lemon juice
Salt and freshly ground pepper to taste
1/2 cup vegetable or olive oil

IN A SMALL BOWL, whisk vinegar or lemon juice, salt, and pepper together until salt dissolves. Whisk in oil. Taste and add more salt and pepper if needed. Cover and refrigerate for up to 1 week.

MUSTARD VINAIGRETTE

Use on salads with assertive greens.

1 teaspoon Dijon mustard

2 tablespoons red or white wine vinegar

Salt and freshly ground pepper to taste

1 clove garlic, minced

$\frac{1}{2}$ cup olive or vegetable oil

IN A SMALL BOWL, whisk mustard, vinegar, salt, pepper, and garlic together. Gradually whisk in oil in a fine stream.

CREAMY HERB VINAIGRETTE

makes about ³⁄₄ cup

Use on tomato salads.

1 tablespoon fresh lemon juice

2 tablespoons red or white wine vinegar

1 teaspoon minced fresh herbs such as tarragon,
   dill, parsley, thyme

2 tablespoons heavy cream or sour cream

Salt and freshly ground pepper to taste

6 tablespoons olive or vegetable oil

IN A SMALL BOWL, whisk lemon juice, vinegar, herbs, cream or sour cream, salt, and pepper together. Gradually whisk in oil.

RASPBERRY-SHALLOT VINAIGRETTE

Use on poultry salads, assertive greens, and green bean salads.

1 tablespoon minced shallot

3 tablespoons raspberry vinegar

Salt and freshly ground pepper to taste

$^1/_4$ cup vegetable oil

$^1/_4$ cup walnut oil

IN A SMALL BOWL, whisk shallot, vinegar, salt, and pepper together. Gradually whisk in vegetable and walnut oils.

SHERRY-ORANGE VINAIGRETTE

makes about 1/2 cup

Use on greens with fruit, seafood, and poultry.

2 tablespoons fresh orange juice

2 tablespoons sherry vinegar

Salt and freshly ground pepper to taste

¹/₂ cup olive oil

1 tablespoon nonpareil capers, drained and rinsed

IN A SMALL BOWL, whisk orange juice, vinegar, salt, and pepper together. Gradually whisk in oil. Stir in capers.

A **MAYONNAISE** MEDLEY

This homemade mayonnaise makes a delicious, simple dressing that can be quickly sparked with the additions that follow.

BASIC MAYONNAISE

makes about 1½ cups

2 egg yolks
1 teaspoon Dijon mustard
2 teaspoons fresh lemon juice
1 to 1½ cups vegetable oil
Salt and freshly ground pepper to taste

IN A BLENDER or food processor, combine all ingredients except oil and process until well blended. With machine running, add oil in a slow, steady stream. Mixture will thicken. For a light mayonnaise, use 1 cup oil; for a richer, thicker mayonnaise, 1½ cups oil.

FLAVORED MAYONNAISES

Even if you don't make mayonnaise from scratch, a good-quality store-bought mayo can be turned into a flavorful dressing.

HERB MAYONNAISE: Add ½ cup chopped fresh herbs to 1 cup mayonnaise.

GARLIC MAYONNAISE: Crush 2 or 3 cloves garlic with a garlic press and add to 1 cup mayonnaise.

SHERRY MAYONNAISE: Add 1 tablespoon sherry vinegar to 1 cup mayonnaise.

TOMATO MAYONNAISE: Add 4 chopped oil-packed sun-dried tomatoes to 1 cup mayonnaise.

MUSTARD MAYONNAISE: Add 3 tablespoons hot-sweet mustard to 1 cup mayonnaise.

HORSERADISH MAYONNAISE: Add 2 tablespoons grated fresh horseradish or prepared white horseradish to 1 cup mayonnaise.

SALAD SAVVY

Salads may be the one area of life were technology has intruded minimally. A few things, however, are worth mentioning.

BOWLS: When making salad for more than 4 people, we like to toss the salad in large (really large) stainless-steel bowls. We then transfer the dressed salad to a large shallow pasta bowl for serving. The force of gravity makes excess dressing pool in the bottom of deep bowls. Try this method for making salad ahead of time: In a shallow salad serving bowl, whisk dressing ingredients together. Leave the tossers in the bowl and place the salad greens over them. You can let salad stand this way for up to 1 hour. Just before serving, toss well.

BLENDER: Makes quick work of puréeing and of emulsifying salad dressing.

FOOD PROCESSOR: Excellent for grating and shredding cheeses and vegetables and combining dressing ingredients. If you make a lot of slaws, a food processor is a life-saver.

GARLIC PRESS: This tool purées garlic cloves to whisk into dressing without having to chop them. Make sure you buy a sturdy one.

MORTAR AND PESTLE: Indispensable equipment for crushing and grinding small amounts of seeds, spices, and herbs. Make sure the mortar has a rough grinding surface for better friction while grinding.

PEPPERMILL: Essential for salad making and for that final fresh taste at the table.

SALAD SPINNER: This gadget comes in many forms and works exceptionally well for drying washed greens.

SALAD TOSSERS AND SERVERS: For large amounts of salad, a clean pair of hands are most adept. An alternate to human hands are short wooden tossers (shaped like hands) called Salad Hands. Spring-lock tongs make excellent salad servers.

WIRE WHISK: An 8-inch stainless-steel sauce whisk blends dressing ingredients efficiently.

ZESTER: This gadget makes fine shreds of citrus zest in seconds.

02

BITE-SIZED
SALADS

BITE-SIZED

THESE BEFORE-DINNER treats include hand-held hors d'oeuvres, appetizers, and tidbits. No more than a bite or two, these tantalizing mini-salads have the usual preprandial purpose of stimulating the palate for the meal to come. But what makes them truly irresistible is their ease of preparation.

SALADS

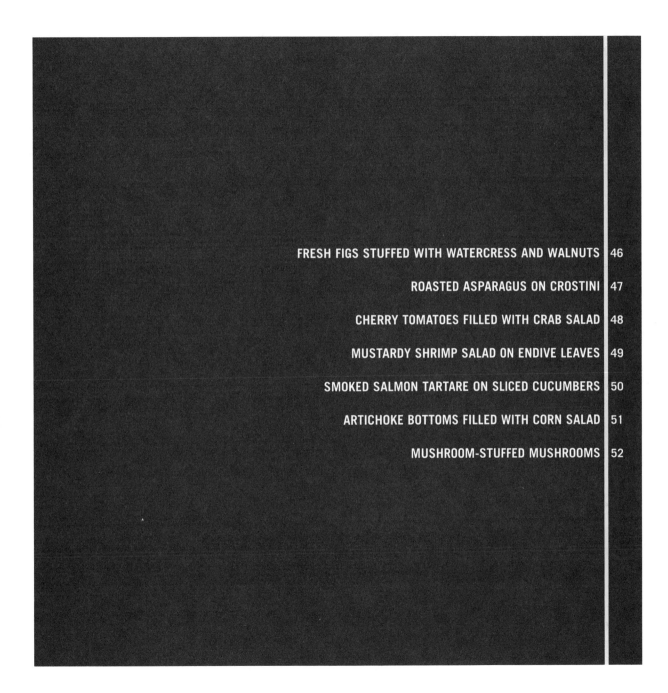

FRESH FIGS STUFFED
WITH WATERCRESS AND WALNUTS

makes > 16 stuffed figs

A few summers ago, figs started to remind us a little of zucchini—not in taste, of course, but in proliferation. Everyone, it seemed, offered fruit bowls spilling over with figs of all description, thanks to an excess of enthusiasm at farmer's markets. Who could resist the plump, luscious Calimyrnas, the deep-purple Missions, or any other variety of these short-season fruits at their prime? Not us, which explains this succulent summer morsel, its sweetness set off by the pungency of watercress and the crunch of walnuts.

1 bunch watercress, stemmed and coarsely chopped

1 cup (4 ounces) walnuts, toasted and coarsely
   chopped (see page 32)

3 tablespoons snipped fresh chives

1/2 teaspoon salt

Pinch of cayenne pepper

2 tablespoons plain yogurt or sour cream

3 tablespoons mayonnaise

1 teaspoon fresh lemon juice

16 fresh green or black figs

IN A MEDIUM BOWL, combine all ingredients except figs. Stand figs upright and, with scissors, cut an **X** through tops. Gently pull 4 sections apart, creating a cavity in each fig. Fill each fig with about 1 tablespoon watercress mixture. Serve at room temperature or chilled.

VARIATION: To serve as a sit-down, knife-and-fork, salad course: Dress 8 cups seasonal greens with Mustard Vinaigrette (see page 34). Place mound of greens on a serving plate and top with 2 stuffed figs.

ROASTED ASPARAGUS ON CROSTINI

makes 16 crostini

Neither fat nor thin but somewhere in between—that's the preferred asparagus body type when it comes to roasting. A few minutes at high heat adds a caramelized note, conserves the right amount of crunch, and coaxes out the vegetable's deepest flavors. Best of all, the roasting can be done hours in advance of the final assembly.

1¹/₂ pounds medium asparagus, trimmed

3 tablespoons extra-virgin olive oil

1 teaspoon salt

¹/₄ teaspoon ground pepper

1 tablespoon fresh lemon juice

16 Garlic Crostini (see page 31)

16 strips roasted red pepper (see page 32)

PREHEAT OVEN to 450°F. Cut asparagus into 2-inch lengths. Place in a medium bowl and toss with oil, salt, and pepper. Spread on nonstick or lightly greased baking sheet. Roast for about 15 minutes, or until slightly browned. Let cool completely and sprinkle with lemon juice. Taste and adjust seasoning if necessary. Place 3 or 4 asparagus pieces on each toast. Top with a red pepper strip.

CHERRY TOMATOES
FILLED WITH CRAB SALAD

"Stars of the earth"—that's what Pablo Neruda called tomatoes, marveling at how they impart to salads their "fresh, deep, inexhaustible sun." Bright orange, yellow, or red cherry tomatoes also make beautiful little bowls for single-bite treats like this one. The sweet crab filling, accented with mustard and green peppercorns, can also be a delicious light lunch, served on greens or spread on toasted sourdough.

1 pound fresh lump crabmeat, picked over for shell

2 teaspoons green peppercorns, rinsed and lightly crushed

¼ cup snipped fresh chives

¼ cup chopped fresh parsley

1 tablespoon snipped fresh dill

¼ cup mayonnaise

2 teaspoons fresh lemon juice

1 tablespoon sweet-hot mustard

Salt and freshly ground pepper to taste

32 medium to large cherry tomatoes (assorted colors would be lovely)

IN A LARGE BOWL, combine crabmeat, peppercorns, chives, parsley, and dill. In small bowl, combine mayonnaise, lemon juice, and mustard. Mix with crabmeat and add salt and pepper. May be refrigerated, covered, for up to 12 hours if not using immediately. **CUT ABOUT** ¼ inch off blossom end of tomatoes with a serrated knife. To make tomatoes sit upright without tipping over, you may have to cut a very thin slice from bottom. Scoop out seeds with a tiny teaspoon (an espresso spoon works very well) and discard. Sprinkle cavities with a bit of salt and place upside down on 2 layers of paper towels for 1 hour. **GENEROUSLY FILL** cavities with crabmeat salad. Refrigerate for up to 2 hours. Serve cold or at room temperature.

MUSTARDY SHRIMP SALAD ON ENDIVE LEAVES

Honey mustard may be relatively new to our palates, but the Romans were hot on its trail. Among the recipes of Apicius, dating from around 1 B.C., is an endive salad with honey in the dressing to offset the vegetable's bitterness. Use endives in winter salads, he counsels, when "real lettuce" is not available. Hmmm . . . maybe we have come a long way since Apicius.

2 tablespoons mustard seeds

2 tablespoons vegetable oil

3 tablespoons capers, drained and rinsed

$1/2$ red bell pepper, seeded, deribbed, and diced

$1/2$ cup chopped fresh parsley

2 tablespoons Dijon mustard

$1/4$ cup mayonnaise

$1/4$ cup plain yogurt or sour cream

1 tablespoon fresh lemon juice

1 teaspoon minced fresh tarragon, or $1/2$ teaspoon dried tarragon

1 pound bay shrimp

Salt and freshly ground pepper to taste

6 heads Belgian endive

1 bunch watercress, stemmed and coarsely chopped

IN A SMALL SKILLET over medium high heat, heat oil and cook mustard seeds until they pop. Let cool, then mix with capers, pepper, parsley, mustard, mayonnaise, yogurt, lemon juice, and tarragon until well combined. Add shrimp and mix gently. Add salt and pepper. **COARSELY CHOP** 1 endive and toss with watercress. Moisten with about 2 tablespoons mayonnaise mixture. Core and separate leaves of the remaining 5 endives. Select 36 of the best-looking leaves and place about 1 tablespoon shrimp salad on pointed end. Mound watercress mixture in center of serving platter and surround with filled endive leaves.

SMOKED SALMON TARTARE
ON SLICED CUCUMBERS

Never hurry a cucumber. Give it a chance. Slice into it as you would a melon: expectantly, breathing in its crisp fragrance, its provocative subtlety. Carved into thin slices and paved with smoked salmon, the cucumber complies beautifully. Not passive or docile, it contributes just the right clarity, part of a perfect match.

SMOKED SALMON TARTARE:

8 ounces smoked salmon

1 small red onion

2 tablespoons fresh lemon juice

2 tablespoons extra-virgin olive oil

Salt and freshly ground pepper to taste

2 tablespoons capers, drained and rinsed

1 tablespoon snipped fresh dill

1 English (hothouse) cucumber, sliced ¼ inch thick

2 tablespoons Dijon mustard

Tiny dill sprigs for garnish

TO MAKE TARTARE: In a blender or food processor, process smoked salmon, onion, lemon juice, and olive oil to a rough paste. Add salt and pepper and stir in capers and dill. **SPREAD CUCUMBER SLICES** with a thin film of mustard. Top each with about 1 teaspoon salmon tartare. Garnish each slice with a sprig of dill.

ARTICHOKE BOTTOMS
FILLED WITH CORN SALAD

The artichoke centennial is upon us! The year 2000 will commemorate the first planting of arti-chokes in this country, specifically around Half Moon Bay in Northern California and on down to Castroville, now the nation's major producer. This represents quite a conquest for these thistle-covered "monstrous productions of the earth," as Pliny referred to them. Here, a tiny scoop of sugar-sweet corn helps show off the artichoke's natural nutlike charms to delicious advantage. In artichoke anatomy, by the way, bottoms are the same as hearts, just one of the artichoke's unexpected traits.

16 small artichokes

1 lemon, halved

CORN SALAD:

1 cup fresh corn kernels (about 2 ears)

$^1/_2$ cup diced roasted red pepper (see page 32)

2 tablespoons capers, drained and rinsed

2 tablespoons Mustard Mayonnaise (page 39)

Salt and freshly ground pepper to taste

Parsley sprigs for garnish

TO PREPARE ARTICHOKE bottoms, cut off stems and discard. Remove leaves until you reach pale yellow-green ones. Cut off top two thirds of each artichoke. With a tiny spoon, scrape out fuzzy choke and rub artichokes with lemon halves. Place artichoke bottoms in a large pot of water with lemon halves. Bring to a boil, reduce heat, and simmer for about 7 minutes, or until tender. Drain and let cool. **COOK CORN** in salted boiling water for 3 minutes. Drain and let cool. Combine all ingredients for corn salad. Spoon into artichoke bottoms. Garnish each with a parsley sprig.

MUSHROOM-STUFFED MUSHROOMS

makes 12 stuffed mushrooms

Fungusheads—that's what a friend of ours calls those of us who become misty-eyed about mushrooms. We can't help it, because as playthings for the senses, mushrooms have it all: a musky fragrance, an exquisitely touchable flesh, an easy compatibility with so many other ingredients, a willing transformation into the state of voluptuousness. A recipe like this is not for fence sitters—it's strictly for fungusheads.

FILLING:

2 tablespoons butter

2 shallots, minced

1 pound cremini or white mushrooms, chopped

$^1\!/_2$ cup chopped fresh parsley

2 tablespoons snipped fresh dill

$1^1\!/_2$ teaspoons minced fresh tarragon, or

   $^1\!/_2$ teaspoon dried tarragon

$^1\!/_8$ teaspoon cayenne pepper

2 tablespoons tomato paste

$^1\!/_4$ cup heavy cream

Salt and freshly ground pepper to taste

12 cremini mushrooms, stemmed

Olive oil for brushing

12 pieces fresh chives

TO MAKE FILLING: In a medium skillet, melt butter over medium heat and sauté shallots until soft, about 4 minutes. Stir in chopped mushrooms and cook until liquid evaporates, about 6 minutes. Add all remaining filling ingredients. Cook until mixture thickens slightly, 3 to 4 minutes. In a blender or food processor, process until mixture forms a coarse paste. Taste and adjust seasoning. **PREHEAT BROILER.** Brush mushroom caps with oil and broil for about 4 minutes, or until slightly soft. Let cool. Fill caps with mushroom filling. Arrange 2 pieces of chives in an **X** on each cap.

03
STARTER SALADS

THESE SALAD combinations are deftly seasoned to intrigue and awaken the palate. Although there is a variety to fit the style of any meal, they all have one thing in common: the unhindered natural flavors of fresh ingredients. They are quickly prepared and assembled, making them as inviting to the cook as to the guest.

FENNEL AND APPLE SALAD
WITH APPLE VINAIGRETTE
AND TOASTED HAZELNUTS

Apples as symbols have a heavy workload. They are the stuff of childhood lunch boxes and the American pie filling of mythic proportions; they mean cider in autumn and applesauce all winter long. They have always been generous with possibility, so we knew we could count on them as the foundation for this fruit vinaigrette. Puréed apples emulsify, thicken, and sweeten this mustard-spiked dressing; and they transform a bowlful of spinach into a memory.

APPLE VINAIGRETTE:

¹/₂ tart green apple, peeled, cored, and chopped

1 tablespoon minced shallots

1 teaspoon mild mustard

1 teaspoon honey

¹/₄ cup cider vinegar

¹/₂ cup olive oil

Salt and freshly ground pepper to taste

2 fennel bulbs, trimmed, cored, and thinly sliced

4 tart-sweet red apples, cored and thinly sliced

4 cups young spinach leaves

1 cup (4 ounces) hazelnuts, toasted, skinned, and coarsely chopped (see page 32)

1 cup (4 ounces) shredded Vermont Cheddar cheese

IN A BLENDER or food processor, combine all vinaigrette ingredients and process until emulsified. In a large bowl, combine fennel, apples, spinach, and hazelnuts. Toss well with vinaigrette and sprinkle with cheese.

PARSLEY AND RAW MUSHROOM SALAD WITH CHIVE VINAIGRETTE

Over the years, parsley has been extremely patient. Because of its green good looks, it has been used as a mere decoration, often on edibles less worthy than itself. It has been included in many a dish only to be cast to the rim of the plate when the real eating began. And then, a few years back, salads started to become the stars of the meal; everything green was golden, including parsley. People began to realize that there was something wholesome and honest about parsley, like walking through a country meadow at dawn or breathing fresh-mown hay. Finally, parsley became a salad in itself. Here is one of its interesting possibilities. We suggest flat-leaf, as opposed to curly parsley, because of its more robust flavor.

CHIVE VINAIGRETTE:

2 tablespoons fresh lemon juice

1 clove garlic, crushed

$1/4$ cup finely snipped fresh chives

$1/4$ cup extra-virgin olive oil

$1/2$ teaspoon ground pepper

$1/4$ teaspoon salt

4 cups flat-leaf parsley leaves (about 2 good-sized bunches)

8 cremini mushrooms, very thinly sliced

$1/4$ cup grated Parmesan cheese

WHISK ALL vinaigrette ingredients together until well blended, or process in a blender or food processor. (Latter method will purée chives, giving dressing a lovely green color.) **IN A LARGE BOWL,** combine parsley and mushrooms and toss with vinaigrette. Sprinkle with Parmesan cheese.

GREENS AND GRAPEFRUIT
WITH GOAT CHEESE DRESSING
AND CARAMELIZED PECANS

It takes just a few minutes to caramelize the pecans for this salad, and gratification is almost instant. The aroma of toasted nuts is the initial reward, but only when the salad is complete do the pecans reveal the fullness of their charms. Simultaneously sweet, salty, peppery, crunchy, and buttery, they coax every last taste bud into action. Add a few greens, some grapefruit, and goat cheese, and you have an exciting beginning to your meal.

1 cup (4 ounces) pecans, coarsely chopped

1/4 cup sugar

1/4 teaspoon salt

1/4 teaspoon ground pepper

DRESSING:

2 tablespoons fresh white goat cheese at room
    temperature

2 tablespoons fresh orange juice

2 tablespoons fresh lemon juice

1/2 teaspoon dried thyme

2 tablespoons olive oil

5 cups mixed salad greens, torn into bite-sized
    pieces

1 pink grapefruit, peeled and sectioned (see
    page 32)

IN A MEDIUM nonstick skillet, toast pecans over medium-high heat until they just begin to color. Sprinkle with sugar and stir until sugar melts and coats nuts. Transfer to a flat plate and sprinkle with salt and pepper. Let cool. **IN A SMALL BOWL,** combine all dressing ingredients and whisk until smooth. In large bowl, combine greens and grapefruit. Toss with dressing and top with pecans.

ENDIVE, WATERCRESS, AND BLOOD ORANGE SALAD

A bad hair day? A hectic week at the office? This salad might be just the antidote. A combination of oil, vinegar, and endive, the basis of a classic headache remedy, is the foundation of this colorful dish. Its panoply of bitter, peppery, and sweet is downright provocative to most guests, no matter their mood. And it tastes a lot better than aspirin.

2 heads Belgian endive, cored and cut into fine
    shreds

4 cups watercress leaves (about 1 large bunch)

2 blood oranges, peeled and sectioned (see page 32)

1 small red onion, diced

1/2 cup imported black olives, halved and pitted

DRESSING:

3 tablespoons sherry vinegar

2 tablespoons walnut oil

1/4 cup olive oil

2 teaspoons finely chopped fresh parsley

Salt and freshly ground pepper to taste

IN A LARGE BOWL, combine endive, watercress, orange sections, onion, and olives. In a small bowl, whisk vinegar, walnut oil, olive oil, and parsley together until well blended. Toss with salad and add salt and pepper.

SPINACH SALAD WITH PERSIMMONS AND DRIED CRANBERRIES

If Popeye were just starting out, he'd have something new to bring to a spinach-skeptical world. Spinach salads have probably won more converts in recent times than any single class of traditional spinach dishes. Because they accommodate a variety of ingredients—meats, vegetables, all types of cheeses, and nuts—spinach salads please many palates. This version, with sweet slices of Fuyu persimmons, dried cranberries, and a whisper of curry, offers both the exotic and familiar.

6 cups young spinach leaves, torn into bite-sized
  pieces

1 bunch scallions, thinly sliced

2 Fuyu persimmons, cut into $1/2$-inch wedges

1 cup dried cranberries, soaked in 1 cup hot water
  for 1 hour

DRESSING:

1 teaspoon curry powder

2 tablespoons reserved cranberry soaking liquid
  (above)

2 tablespoons fresh lemon juice

1 tablespoon balsamic vinegar

$3/4$ cup olive oil

Salt and freshly ground pepper to taste

$1/2$ cup unsweetened shredded coconut for garnish

IN A LARGE BOWL, combine spinach, scallions, and persimmon wedges. Drain cranberries, reserving 2 tablespoons soaking liquid, and add to spinach mixture. **IN A SMALL BOWL,** whisk curry powder, reserved cranberry soaking liquid, lemon juice, vinegar, and olive oil together. Add salt and pepper. Toss with spinach mixture and garnish with coconut.

SHREDDED BEETS AND APPLES ON ARUGULA

Any dish containing beets brings up an age-old dilemma: What is the best way to transform beets from raw to cooked? In an old French recipe, Julia Child once discovered instructions to cook beets under an earthenware bowl set on dampened straw until "shriveled and charred." Elizabeth David cautions that beets should be purchased already cooked "from a greengrocer who cooks them carefully, which is none too common." Perhaps the oldest counsel we uncovered is from John Gerard's sixteenth-century *Herball, or General Histoire of Plantes.* He wrote that the beet "eaten when it is boyled . . . nourishes little or nothing, and is not so wholesome as lettuce." We've tried to avoid the above pitfalls by roasting beets in foil, which helps to retain the sweet, earthy flavor that is this salad's main attraction.

2 large beets (red or gold or both), roasted and
    shredded (see Note)
2 tart apples, peeled, cored, and shredded
½ cup snipped fresh chives

DRESSING:
2 tablespoons heavy cream
2 tablespoons fresh lemon juice
2 tablespoons fresh orange juice

1 teaspoon honey
1 tablespoon coarsely chopped fresh mint
Salt and freshly ground pepper to taste

4 cups arugula
4 fresh mint leaves for garnish

IN A MEDIUM BOWL, combine beets, apples, and chives. In a small bowl, whisk all dressing ingredients together. Toss two thirds of dressing with beet mixture. Toss remaining dressing with arugula. **ON 4 SERVING PLATES,** make a bed of arugula. Top with beet mixture and garnish with a mint leaf.

ROASTING BEETS: Preheat oven to 425°F. Wrap each beet in aluminum foil and roast for 45 minutes to 1 hour, or until easily pierced with the tip of a knife. Let cool to the touch. Peel while still warm.

WILTED CUCUMBER SALAD
WITH SCALLIONS AND RADISHES

In his masterpiece, *Of Time and the River,* Thomas Wolfe writes lustily of "a speared forkful of those thin-sliced cucumbers—ah! what a delicate and toothsome pickle they do make—what sorcerer invented them . . . " **Ironically,** those less enthusiastic about the vegetable have resorted to various forms of sorcery to extract some flavor from cucumbers. The Romans, who discovered the cucumber in Asia and successfully transplanted it, tried a variety of potions. Roman cooks seasoned it with everything from pennyroyal to sylphium, an expensive though suspicious-sounding flavoring. They boiled the bland vegetable with precooked brains (presumably animal brains) and added honey and cumin at serving time. Something must have worked, because we know that Emperor Tiberius liked cucumbers so much he had them grown in carts that could be wheeled out for a daily sun bath to help them thrive, even off-season. **Our methods** are less physically demanding: a sprinkle of salt and a firm hand to press out the liquid and help soften the slices. Those who prefer their cucumbers crisp can soak the slices in ice water prior to serving.

1 English (hothouse) cucumber, thinly sliced

Salt for sprinkling

4 scallions, trimmed and thinly sliced

8 red radishes, thinly sliced

1 small head iceberg lettuce

DRESSING:

1/2 cup plain yogurt

1 clove garlic, minced

1 teaspoon honey or sugar

1 1/2 teaspoons minced fresh tarragon, or
   1/2 teaspoon dried tarragon

2 tablespoons olive oil

1/2 teaspoon salt

1/2 teaspoon ground pepper

IN A COLANDER, layer the cucumber slices with salt and let stand about 30 minutes. Pour off liquid that has formed and press cucumbers firmly. **IN A LARGE BOWL,** toss cucumbers with scallions and radishes. Cut the lettuce in half through the core. Slice lettuce in $\frac{1}{2}$-inch shreds and toss with cucumber mixture. Combine all dressing ingredients and whisk to blend. Toss with cucumber salad. Serve immediately.

CORN, RADISH,
AND PARSLEY SALAD

As a salad ingredient, radishes have a long, venerable past. The Chinese, for example, make a traditional New Year's dish of julienned radish and dried apricots accompanied with a sweet and sour sauce. The German Rettichsalat is a white radish salad often paired with steak. In England, radishes were once the symbol of spring and were consumed, along with English ale, in festive quantities during the traditional May Radish Feast. This parsley-based salad balances the sweetness of fat corn kernels with the bright attention-getting tingle of radishes.

DRESSING:

2 scallions, cut into small pieces

1 tablespoon hot-sweet mustard

1 1/2 teaspoons fresh thyme, or 1/2 teaspoon dried
   thyme

2 tablespoons champagne vinegar

6 tablespoons grapeseed oil or other light oil

2 cups fresh corn kernels (about 4 ears)

8 red radishes, chopped

4 cups minced fresh flat-leaf parsley

Salt and freshly ground pepper to taste

COMBINE dressing ingredients in a food processor or blender and process until smooth. Cook corn in salted boiling water for 3 minutes. Drain and let cool. In a large bowl, combine corn, radishes, and parsley. Toss with dressing. Add salt and pepper.

GREENS AND GRAPES

serves > 4

In this treasure hunt of a salad, wondrous enticements lie in wait amid the tangle of watercress and lettuce. Crumbled bits of Roquefort and toasted nuts interact with their usual appeal, but the real irresistibles are the grapes. Almost any variety will do, but a mix of colors—from translucent green and deep burgundy to silvery black—makes this salad an even more sparkling beginning to a meal.

2 cups watercress leaves

2 cups butter lettuce leaves, torn into bite-sized
   pieces

1 cup seedless grapes

$1/2$ cup (2 ounces) pine nuts, toasted

$1/2$ cup (2 ounces) crumbled Roquefort cheese

3 tablespoons balsamic vinegar

6 tablespoons extra-virgin olive oil

$1/2$ teaspoon mild mustard

Salt and freshly ground pepper to taste

IN A MEDIUM BOWL, combine watercress, lettuce, grapes, pine nuts, and cheese. Whisk vinegar, oil, and mustard together. Toss with salad. Add salt and pepper.

FRISÉE AND WATERCRESS
WITH NECTARINE NUGGETS

With nuts and fruit, greens and olives, this salad has a lot going on both in taste and texture. But what makes it so welcome as the start to a meal is the mouth-tingling bite of watercress. Unique among salad greens, watercress has a kind of cool heat that clears and refreshes the palate and makes it eager for new sensations. Its mustardy crunch has made it popular both raw and cooked, in salads and soups, with discriminating diners and with hikers passing by cress-lined rivers and streams.

3 cups frisée lettuce, torn into bite-sized pieces

3 cups watercress leaves

3 nectarines, halved, pitted, and cut into ¼-inch cubes

½ cup imported black olives, halved and pitted

½ cup (2 ounces) walnut halves, toasted (see page 32)

DRESSING:

3 tablespoons raspberry vinegar

¼ cup walnut oil

¼ cup olive oil

Salt and freshly ground pepper to taste

IN A LARGE BOWL, combine frisée, watercress, nectarines, olives, and walnuts. In a small bowl, whisk the vinegar, walnut oil, olive oil, salt, and pepper together. Toss with salad.

SEASONAL GREENS WITH GORGONZOLA DOLCELATTE AND CRISP PANCETTA

serves > 8

Seasonal is the secret word in this salad and in any salad for that matter. In fall and winter, spinach, baby mustard greens, and Belgian endive provide a sturdy background for the pungent mix of cheese and pancetta. Spring and summer offer an array, from arugula and Bibb lettuce to watercress and yuca flowers, depending on location. The important thing, as the English food writer Edward Bunyard warns in *The Epicure's Companion,* is to avoid those out-of-season "limp and soddened leaves, devoid of crispness, resembling a copy of *The Times* which has floated down from Hammersmith to Depford." If you can't find the intriguingly sweet dolcelatte, a young Gorgonzola, substitute any mild blue cheese.

8 cups seasonal greens, torn into bite-sized pieces

4 ounces Gorgonzola dolcelatte, crumbled (about 1 cup)

4 ounces pancetta or bacon, diced

3 tablespoons minced shallots

3 tablespoons balsamic vinegar

$1/3$ cup olive oil

IN A LARGE BOWL, combine the greens and Gorgonzola. **IN A MEDIUM SKILLET** over medium heat, cook pancetta or bacon until fat is rendered. Add shallots and cook until pancetta is crisp and shallots are translucent, about 6 minutes. With a slotted spoon, transfer pancetta and shallots to greens. Add vinegar to skillet and cook for about 1 minute. Remove from heat and whisk in olive oil. Pour over greens and toss well.

WARM ASPARAGUS WITH
LEMON AND PARMESAN

Put this quintessentially Italian salad together on a warm spring afternoon and you may feel like you're cheating. For all that lusty Tuscan flavor—the olive oil, the Parmesan, the asparagus—there is almost nothing to do. Nothing but good ingredients tossed with each other, this dish is pure simplicity. You can taste it.

2 pounds thin asparagus

2 tablespoons fresh lemon juice

3 tablespoons extra-virgin olive oil

$^1/_2$ cup (2 ounces) freshly grated Parmigiano-
   Reggiano cheese

Salt and freshly ground pepper to taste

IN A LARGE POT of boiling water, cook asparagus for 2 minutes. Drain and arrange on a platter. While still warm, sprinkle asparagus with lemon juice, olive oil, cheese, salt, and pepper.

GRILLED PORTOBELLO, SPINACH, AND CORN SALAD

No doubt about it: Portobellos have a flair for the dramatic. Whether served whole or cut into long, velvety strips, they add a "can't wait" dimension to any dish. And perhaps no other mushroom qualifies so completely for the nickname "vegetable meat," a term referring to its dense, substantial nature. Here, the contrast of raw and cooked makes a simple spinach salad an exciting start to any meal.

4 portobello mushrooms, stemmed

7 tablespoons olive oil

Salt and freshly ground pepper to taste

4 cups baby spinach leaves

3 cups fresh corn kernels (about 6 ears)

3 tablespoons sherry vinegar

COOK corn in boiling salted water for three minutes. Drain and let cool. **WITH A SHARP KNIFE,** cut slits in top and underside of each mushroom cap. Brush tops and bottoms with $1^{1}/_{2}$ tablespoons of oil and sprinkle with salt and pepper. Light a fire in a charcoal grill or preheat a gas grill or a broiler. Grill or broil mushrooms for about 4 minutes on each side. Let cool and cut into $^{1}/_{4}$-inch strips. **IN A LARGE BOWL,** combine mushrooms, spinach, and corn. In a small bowl, whisk together remaining $5^{1}/_{2}$ tablespoons oil and vinegar. Toss with salad.

ZUCCHINI CARPACCIO

Although carpaccio is usually associated with uncooked beef, salmon, or tuna, it is not altogether erroneous to use the term for this artistically arranged dish. Originally made with beef, the dish was created at Harry's Bar in Venice in honor of Vittorio Carpaccio, a fifteenth-century Venetian painter. (Another theory contends that Carpaccio's name was used with raw dishes because his work was characterized by touches of red.) We borrowed the name for this molded raw zucchini salad served, for color, on slices of tomato.

6 young firm zucchini, coarsely shredded
³/₄ cup (3 ounces) shredded Parmesan cheese
10 fresh basil leaves, cut into thin shreds
1 garlic clove, minced
3 tablespoons fresh lemon juice
2 tablespoons olive oil
Salt and freshly ground pepper to taste
6 Roma (plum) tomatoes

SQUEEZE EXCESS water from zucchini. In a large bowl, combine zucchini, cheese, half the basil, garlic, lemon juice, oil, salt, and pepper. Taste and adjust seasoning. Pack mixture into six 4-ounce ramekins. Refrigerate for at least 1 hour or up to 3 hours. **CUT** each tomato lengthwise into 6 slices. On each of 6 salad plates, arrange 6 slices in a circle. Unmold zucchini in center of plates and sprinkle with remaining basil.

GINGERED GOLDEN BEET SALAD

serves • 6

Coconut milk adds a fusion touch to this marinated vegetable starter. Once an exotic ingredient, a staple in Indonesian and Thai cuisines, coconut milk is now available in many supermarkets, where it is sold unsweetened in cans, usually grouped with Asian foods. The best Thai brands, containing nothing but grated coconut meat and water, sport the word *gata,* which designates a particularly rich and excellent product.

$^1/_2$ **cup fresh orange juice**

1 tablespoon grated fresh ginger

$^1/_2$ **teaspoon ground cinnamon**

**4 golden beets, cooked, peeled, and shredded (see
     page 63)**

2 zucchini, shredded

$^1/_3$ **cup coconut milk**

$^2/_3$ **cup plain yogurt**

Fresh mint leaves for garnish

IN A SMALL BOWL, combine orange juice, ginger, and cinnamon. In a large bowl, combine beets and zucchini. Toss with juice mixture. Let sit for about 2 hours. Pour off excess liquid. **IN A SMALL BOWL,** combine yogurt and coconut milk and toss with salad. Garnish with mint.

NOTES

FOLK SALADS

THESE RECIPES, INSPIRED BY OLD-WORLD TRADITIONS AND AMERICAN REGIONAL DISHES, HAVE BEEN REFINED FOR CONTEMPORARY TASTES. THEY MAKE USE OF SPECIAL INGREDIENTS—SPICES, CHEESES, AND PRODUCE—THAT GIVE THEM CHARACTER AND APPEAL. ROOTED IN CULTURE AND CUSTOM, THEY PROVOKE MEMORIES AS WELL AS TASTE BUDS.

SALADS

PANZANELLA

Everything about this dish is fun, especially all the speculation about its name and origins. Made from stale country bread and tomatoes, it is a peasant dish usually attributed to Tuscany or Rome. The name either means "little swamp" (according to Waverly Root, who traces it to Rome), or "little soup tureen" (from Tuscany), per Carol Field; or it may come from the Roman word *panza,* meaning "belly" (from *Italian Cooking in the Grand Tradition* by Jo Bettoja and Anna Maria Cornetto). Recipes for this salad are plentiful, though somehow, as with so many humble dishes, the results are always tasty and sustaining. Cubes of scamorza, the Italian smoked mozzarella that usually comes in a braid, make this version downright exciting.

1-pound loaf Italian country bread, sliced 1 inch thick

1 red onion, thinly sliced

1 English (hothouse) cucumber, peeled, seeded, and sliced

6 ripe tomatoes, diced

20 fresh basil leaves, cut into thin strips

1 cup Italian black olives, pitted and halved

3 ounces scamorza cheese (smoked mozzarella), cut into $^1/_2$-inch cubes (about $^3/_4$ cup)

$^1/_3$ cup extra-virgin olive oil

3 tablespoons red wine vinegar

Salt and freshly ground pepper to taste

IN A LARGE BOWL, soak bread in cold water to cover for 3 minutes. Squeeze out excess water and tear bread into small pieces. Put in a large salad bowl with onion, cucumber, tomatoes, basil, olives, and cheese. In a small bowl, whisk oil and vinegar together. Toss with salad and add salt and pepper.

FATTOUSH

A close cousin to panzanella, fattoush is a Lebanese dish based on toasted pita bread. As torn bits of pita soak up the juices of diced fresh tomatoes, cucumbers, and lemon, they help bind the ingredients together and transport their flavors. In place of the traditional sumac, an astringent Middle Eastern spice that is not readily accessible, we use cumin for both earthiness and aroma. Garbanzos make this fattoush a substantial meal that can either complement a dinner or, in larger portions, serve as an unusual lunch.

Three 6-inch pita breads, toasted and broken into
  small pieces

$1/2$ cup fresh lemon juice

1 English (hothouse) cucumber, peeled, seeded,
  and diced

4 scallions, thinly sliced

1 red bell pepper, seeded, deribbed, and diced

4 ripe tomatoes, diced

1 cup cooked garbanzo beans (chickpeas)

$1/4$ cup chopped fresh parsley

6 fresh mint leaves, chopped

2 cloves garlic, minced

$1/2$ teaspoon ground cumin

$1/2$ cup olive oil

Salt and freshly ground pepper to taste

IN A LARGE BOWL, moisten pita pieces with 3 tablespoons of lemon juice. Add cucumber, scallions, pepper, tomatoes, beans, parsley, and mint. Toss again. In a small bowl, whisk remaining lemon juice, garlic, cumin, and olive oil together. Toss with salad and add salt and pepper.

CAESAR SALAD

On today's restaurant menus, Caesar salad appears almost as background music. Although it can be ordered for itself, it is often accompanied with options such as chicken, fish, or other ingredients that can transform it into a main course. We see this not as an attempt to bury the traditional Caesar but rather to take advantage of its essential praiseworthy qualities. The primal goodness of olive oil, Parmesan, and romaine, reportedly first assembled at Caesar Cardini's Tijuana restaurant on July 4, 1924, remains the goal of all these innovations, including ours. **If you want** to avoid raw eggs, use 1 tablespoon of mayonnaise instead, a substitute that in no way diminishes the delicious elemental flavor of this American classic.

Leaves from 2 heads romaine lettuce

4 anchovy fillets, mashed

$^1/_2$ teaspoon Dijon mustard

2 cloves garlic, minced

2 tablespoons fresh lemon juice

1 tablespoon best-quality mayonnaise, or 1 egg
   yolk, coddled for 30 to 60 seconds

$^1/_4$ cup extra-virgin olive oil

$^1/_2$ cup (2 ounces) freshly grated Parmesan cheese

2 cups Garlic Croutons (see page 26)

Salt and freshly ground pepper to taste

SET ASIDE outer romaine leaves and save for another use. Tear remaining romaine into bite-sized pieces and put in a large bowl. **IN A SMALL BOWL,** whisk anchovies, mustard, garlic, lemon juice, mayonnaise or egg, and oil together. Toss with romaine, coating evenly. Add croutons and cheese and toss again. Add salt and pepper.

WALDORF SALAD

A true American classic, Waldorf salad is now over one hundred years old. It was created by the twenty-six-year old mâitre d'hôtel of the majestic Waldorf Hotel, Oscar Tschirky, who served it to the fifteen hundred society swells celebrating the hotel's opening. Today the hotel—now the Waldorf Astoria—has honored their nineteenth-century mâitre d' by naming their contemporary bistro Oscar's. **Consisting of equal** quantities of chopped apples and celery tossed with mayonnaise—someone else threw in the walnuts—the basic recipe has survived all attempts to alter its appealing simplicity. Fannie Farmer, in the 1909 edition of her cookbook, couldn't resist fussing with it, suggesting that the cook "remove tops from red or green apples, scoop out inside pulp . . . Refill shells thus made with the salad, replace tops, and serve on lettuce leaves." To be honest, we succumbed to a bit of tinkering too, cutting the mayo with yogurt, tempering the flavors with some fennel and watercress, adding a sprinkle of cheese. It's both lighter and richer—an apt dish for these contrarian times.

1 tart green apple, peeled, cored, and diced

1 red Delicious apple, peeled, cored, and diced

1 small fennel bulb, trimmed, cored, and diced

1 celery stalk, sliced

1 cup (4 ounces) walnuts, toasted and coarsely chopped (see page 32)

2 cups watercress leaves, coarsely chopped

$^1/_3$ cup mayonnaise

$^1/_3$ cup plain yogurt

1 tablespoon fresh lemon juice

12 butter lettuce leaves

$^3/_4$ cup (3 ounces) ounces Maytag blue cheese, crumbled

IN A LARGE BOWL, combine apples, fennel, celery, walnuts, and watercress. In a small bowl, combine mayonnaise, yogurt, and lemon juice. Toss with salad. Place 2 lettuce leaves on each of 6 salad plates. Mound salad on leaves and sprinkle with blue cheese.

SNAPPER LOUIS

Yes, we have departed drastically from the original Louis by replacing the traditional crab with snapper. But our reasons are honorable: This version is just as delicious with almost any white flaky fish. Besides we didn't have to worry about offending Louis, since no one seems to know exactly who is immortalized in the name of this dish. It was a staple of San Francisco's Solari's restaurant before World War II, according to food historian Evan Jones, but others say it was created at the St. Francis, as reported by cookbook author Helen Evans Brown. The Olympic Club in Seattle and the Bohemian Club in Portland also claim its birthright. Even the recipe is uncertain, although as James Beard phrased it, "there have been many different and many horrible versions." **Here, our favorite** herb trilogy for fish—chives, tarragon, and dill—enlivens the flavor, while the cherry tomatoes make for a pretty presentation.

DRESSING:

¹/₂ cup mayonnaise

¹/₃ cup plain yogurt or sour cream

2 teaspoons prepared horseradish

3 tablespoons bottled chile sauce

¹/₄ cup snipped fresh chives

2 tablespoons minced fresh tarragon leaves

2 tablespoons snipped fresh dill

2 tablespoons fresh lemon juice

Salt and freshly ground pepper to taste

2 tablespoons olive oil

1¹/₂ pounds snapper fillet

1 small head romaine lettuce

2 celery stalks, thinly sliced

2 cups cherry tomatoes, halved

2 hard-cooked eggs, quartered

1 ripe avocado, peeled, pitted, and sliced

IN A SMALL BOWL, combine all dressing ingredients and stir until blended. In a large skillet over medium heat, heat oil and cook snapper for about 3 minutes on each side, or until opaque throughout. **REMOVE ABOUT 8 LEAVES** of romaine and lay them around edge of a serving platter with dark green tops facing out. Coarsely chop remaining leaves and combine with celery and about 3 tablespoons dressing. Place on top of large leaves. Combine snapper with remaining dressing and mound over chopped greens. Garnish platter with cherry tomatoes, eggs, and avocado.

SALAMAGUNDY

Popular in Colonial America, salamagundy is an English dish whose name is derived either from French (*salmigondis,* meaning hodgepodge) or Italian (*salami conditi,* meaning pickled salami). Anchovies and some kind of chopped meat seem to be constants, but other ingredients can include ham, pickled herring, hard-cooked eggs, beef, cucumbers, apples, veal, and nasturtiums, all heaped up on lettuce leaves. Putting things in perspective, Hannah Glasse, in her one-hundred-year-old *Art of Cookery,* says soothingly, "You may always make Salmagundy of such things as you have, according to your fancy." **Ours is a comparatively** simple assemblage, anointed with a vinaigrette in which tomato paste and mustard enhance the flavors. Following tradition, the salad is served mounded on greens—in this case, spinach—but is garnished with nontraditional grapes. For a truly festive finale, we refer again to Mrs. Glasse's instructions: "Put a flower of any sort at the top, or a sprig of myrtle."

VINAIGRETTE:

3 tablespoons balsamic vinegar

1 teaspoon tomato paste

1 teaspoon Dijon mustard

2 teaspoons minced shallot

1/2 cup olive oil

Salt and freshly ground pepper to taste

4 cups spinach leaves, torn into bite-sized pieces

4 cups diced cooked chicken

5 anchovy fillets, chopped

1 small red onion, diced

2 hard-cooked eggs, chopped

1/2 cup minced fresh parsley

1 lemon, thinly sliced

2 cups seedless grapes

IN A SMALL BOWL, whisk all vinaigrette ingredients together. In a medium bowl, toss spinach with about 3 tablespoons of vinaigrette. In a large bowl, combine chicken, anchovies, half of onion, and eggs. Toss with remaining vinaigrette. **ON A SERVING PLATTER,** make a bed of spinach. Mound chicken mixture on top. Sprinkle with remaining onion and parsley. Make a border of lemon slices and grapes.

SALADE À LA RUSSE

A mélange of almost any combination of cooked vegetables constitutes the building blocks of salade à la russe, but the mortar is invariably mayo. In some recipes, the vegetables are marinated in French dressing for awhile before the inevitable mayonnaisation, but the reasons for its Russian reputation are elusive. One explanation might be found in a mayo-bound salad—called "vinegrety"—created by a French chef, Olivier, at the famous Hermitage restaurant in Moscow in the 1880s. **In our harvesty version**, butternut squash and celery root nestle among the cooked vegetables, and diced crisp fennel adds contrast. Rice replaces potatoes, for a change, and we've lightened the dressing with yogurt, but you can use all mayo if you prefer.

$\frac{1}{2}$ cup long-grain rice

1 cup peas

1 cup fresh corn kernels (about 2 ears)

1 carrot, diced

1 cup diced peeled butternut squash

1 cup diced peeled celery root

1 cup diced fennel

$\frac{1}{2}$ cup mayonnaise

$\frac{1}{2}$ cup plain yogurt

1 tablespoon Dijon mustard

2 tablespoons minced shallot

Salt and freshly ground pepper to taste

2 large tomatoes, each cut into 6 wedges

ADD RICE to salted simmering water, cover and cook for 18 minutes. Fluff with a fork and let cool. **COOK PEAS,** corn, and carrots in salted boiling water for 3 minutes. Drain and let cool. **COOK SQUASH** and celery root in salted boiling water for 8 minutes. Drain and let cool. **IN A LARGE BOWL,** combine rice and vegetables. In a medium bowl, stir mayonnaise, yogurt, mustard, shallot, salt, and pepper together until blended. Toss with vegetables. Mound on a serving platter and surround with tomato wedges.

GREEK SALAD

Although this is an easy salad to put together, our real motive for making it as often as we do is the feta cheese. Made from sheep's or goat's milk and soaked in salty brine, feta is a white curd cheese whose name means "slice." Its crumbly texture, which turns creamy on the tongue, and its depth of flavor, so assertive and sensual, are enough raisons d'être for a *horiatiki,* the Greek name for this country-style salad. But this one is especially beautiful, thanks to the mingle of dark, earthy olives—purples, greens, blacks—and crisp slices of red radish. Not surprisingly, Greek oregano enhances the distinctly Hellenic character of this lovely dish.

DRESSING:

6 tablespoons extra-virgin olive oil

3 tablespoons fresh lemon juice

$1/2$ teaspoon dried Greek oregano

1 clove garlic, minced

Leaves from 1 small head romaine lettuce, torn into
bite-sized pieces

1 English (hothouse) cucumber, peeled, halved,
seeded, and sliced

2 large tomatoes, cut into 1-inch chunks

4 scallions, thinly sliced

6 red radishes, sliced

6 fresh mint leaves, torn in half

1 cup assorted imported olives, such as kalamata,
Atalanti, Sicilian, and niçoise, pitted and halved

1 cup (5 ounces) crumbled Greek or Bulgarian feta
cheese

Salt and freshly ground pepper to taste

IN A SMALL BOWL, whisk all dressing ingredients together. In a large bowl, combine remaining ingredients. Toss with dressing. Taste and adjust seasoning.

INSALATA CAPRESE

In Italy, this salad which may (or may not) have originated on the isle of Capri, is ubiquitous. It might even be called insalata inescapable, since it is served almost everywhere in the country and in exactly the same way. With predictable layers of tomato, mozzarella, and basil (the red, white, and green of the Italian flag), it is the "no-surprises" dish in the salad category, a tasty if occasionally boring old reliable. Without deviating wildly from expectations, but with the intention of calling the taste buds to attention, we've extended the role of basil into a full-blown pesto-style dressing. We've taken this audacious step on the theory that a handful of Parmesan and a little garlic never disappointed anyone, at least not in Italy.

1 pound fresh mozzarella cheese,
   sliced $1/4$ inch thick
4 ripe tomatoes, sliced $1/4$ inch thick
1 cup fresh basil leaves
3 tablespoons grated Parmesan cheese
2 tablespoons balsamic vinegar
6 tablespoons extra-virgin olive oil
Salt and freshly ground pepper to taste

ON A SERVING PLATE, alternate slices of mozzarella and tomatoes. Sprinkle with half of basil. **IN A BLENDER** or food processor, blend basil and all remaining ingredients together until smooth. Drizzle over salad.

TABBOULEH

serves 6 to 8

You don't want to fuss too much with tabbouleh. The basic structure of this Middle Eastern classic—nutty bulgur, enlivened with lemon, mint, and parsley and tossed with good juicy tomatoes—is both sturdy and reliable. For our version we tucked in some green peas for sweetness and tiny, dark lentils for added earthiness. Fold in a bit of cooked fish or baby shrimp, and this humble salad becomes a meal. Though often served chilled, tabbouleh is really best at room temperature which allows the full play of all its subtle flavors.

1 cup black (beluga) or French green lentils

2 cups peas

1 cup bulgur wheat

3 large tomatoes, diced

1 large red onion, diced

1 cup chopped fresh parsley

1 large red pepper, seeded, deribbed, and diced

6 fresh mint leaves, coarsely chopped

$1/4$ cup extra-virgin olive oil

$1/4$ cup fresh lemon juice

Salt and freshly ground pepper to taste

Leaves from 1 head romaine lettuce

COOK LENTILS in salted simmering water for about 30 minutes, or until tender. Drain and let cool. **COOK PEAS** in salted boiling water for 3 minutes. Drain and let cool. **MEANWHILE,** in a large bowl, combine bulgur and cold water. Let stand for 30 minutes. Drain through a fine-meshed sieve, gently squeezing out water. Place bulgur in a bowl with lentils, tomatoes, onion, peas, parsley, pepper, and mint. Whisk oil and lemon juice together. Toss with bulgur mixture. Add salt and pepper. On the rim of a serving platter, arrange romaine leaves, round edges out. Mound tabbouleh in center.

CELERY RÉMOULADE

From seed to root, stalk to leaf, celery appears in all its forms in this salad. Shreds of knobby celery root contribute their distinct pungency, while celery stalks provide the crispness they're famous for. We've added celery seed to the rémoulade, a mayonnaise-based sauce traditionally spiked with pickles, capers, and herbs and a long-time companion to celery. Topped off with chopped celery leaves, this is no salad for the celery-shy.

1½ pounds celery root (celeriac), peeled and
   shredded (about 4 cups)

3 celery stalks, thinly sliced

6 tablespoons fresh lemon juice

½ cup mayonnaise

½ cup yogurt or low-fat sour cream

1 tablespoon minced capers

2 tablespoons minced cornichons

2 tablespoons Dijon mustard

1 teaspoon sugar

2 tablespoons minced fresh parsley

1 teaspoon celery seed

Salt and freshly ground pepper to taste

3 tablespoons chopped celery leaves

IN A LARGE BOWL, combine celery root and celery and toss with lemon juice. Let marinate for 1 hour. In a small bowl, combine mayonnaise and yogurt or sour cream. Add capers, cornichons, mustard, sugar, parsley, and celery seed. Toss with celery mixture. Add salt and pepper. Garnish with celery leaves.

VITELLO TONNATO

Yes, we have done a bit of finagling with the traditional tuna salad classic, vitello tonnato. Here it becomes a bona fide salad, complete with radicchio and watercress. And instead of veal, this variation centers on poached chicken breast, which makes it a little more accessible as daily fare. But the dressing exudes authenticity, from anchovies to capers, and brings all the elements deliciously together for one of the most lavishly complimented salads in the book.

3 skinless chicken breasts
2 heads radicchio, cut into strips
1 bunch watercress, stemmed

DRESSING:
$^1/_2$ cup reserved poaching liquid (above)
$6^1/_2$ ounces canned tuna packed in olive oil, drained
6 anchovy fillets, rinsed and patted dry
3 tablespoons capers, drained and rinsed
1 cup mayonnaise
Salt and freshly ground pepper to taste

PUT CHICKEN BREASTS in a pot just large enough to hold them. Add cold water to cover. Bring to a boil, cover, and simmer for 1 minute. Remove from heat and let cool to touch with cover slightly ajar. Remove chicken and reserve $^1/_2$ cup poaching liquid. REMOVE AND DISCARD bones and tear or cut chicken into strips. In a large bowl, combine chicken, radicchio, and watercress. IN A BLENDER or food processor, purée reserved poaching liquid with tuna, anchovies, and 2 tablespoons capers. Stir in mayonnaise and add salt and pepper. Toss with chicken mixture and garnish with remaining capers.

GREEN GODDESS SALAD

The Palace Hotel, which first opened in 1875 and burned down in the 1906 earthquake, only to be rebuilt to its former extravagance, has always epitomized San Francisco at its most opulent. Its chefs, such as Ernest Arbogast and Lucien Heyraud, created lavish dishes for grand occasions and important guests. Among these innovations were Oysters Kirkpatrick—a sizzle of bacon, ketchup, and oysters served on the half shell—dedicated to Col. John C. Kirkpatrick; and Green Goddess dressing, an anchovy-laced, garlicky mayonnaise whipped up in honor of George Arliss, a British actor starring in *The Green Goddess,* a wildly popular play in 1920s San Francisco. **In our** turn-of-the-(twenty-first)-century version, we toss a somewhat lightened chive-tinged mixture with traditional romaine and an array of seafood, always a San Francisco trademark.

1 pound medium shrimp, shelled

8 ounces sea scallops, halved horizontally

DRESSING:

1 clove garlic, minced

$\frac{1}{4}$ cup snipped fresh chives

1 tablespoon anchovy paste

2 tablespoons chopped fresh tarragon

1 tablespoon fresh lemon juice

2 tablespoons white wine vinegar

$\frac{1}{2}$ cup chopped fresh parsley

1 teaspoon capers, drained and rinsed

$\frac{1}{2}$ cup mayonnaise

$\frac{1}{2}$ cup plain yogurt

Salt and freshly ground pepper to taste

Leaves from 1 head romaine, torn into bite-sized
  pieces

8 ounces fresh lump crabmeat

1 lemon, thinly sliced

8 cherry tomatoes, halved

2 chives

COOK SHRIMP and scallops in salted simmering water for 3 minutes. Drain and let cool. In a blender or food processor, combine dressing ingredients until smooth. Taste for salt and pepper. **IN A LARGE,** shallow bowl, combine romaine, shrimp, scallops, and crabmeat. Toss with dressing. Alternate lemon slices and cherry tomato halves around edge of bowl, and criss-cross chives in center.

SALADE NIÇOISE

Even the experts admit that there is no exact recipe for salade niçoise. However, when these same experts provide directions for its assembly, their laissez-faire attitude disappears. Waverley Root, for example, calls this a "salad innocent of lettuce," insists on quartered tomatoes ("if they are sliced, it's not a Salade Niçoise"), and prohibits anything cooked except hard-cooked eggs (which he calls "a rather dubious addition not often permitted in Nice itself"). Elizabeth David is a bit more open-minded about the mix of ingredients as long as they are "put in the bowl in large pieces"; neverthe-less, she advises "there should be garlic in the dressing." Interestingly, she traces the origins of this universally popular salad to pan bania, a Provençal sandwich that people order in cafes while watch-ing a game of boules, always with a bottle of wine close at hand. Not a bad accouterment for any ver-sion of this classic folk salad, including ours.

8 ounces small new potatoes

12 ounces green beans, trimmed

1 red bell pepper, seeded, deribbed, and cut into strips

4 tomatoes, cut into wedges

1 small red onion, thinly sliced

$\frac{1}{2}$ cup niçoise olives, pitted

$\frac{1}{3}$ cup fresh parsley, chopped

Two 6$\frac{1}{2}$-ounce cans tuna packed in olive oil, drained

$\frac{1}{2}$ cup olive oil

1 tablespoon Dijon mustard

3 tablespoons red wine vinegar

2 cloves garlic, minced

Salt and freshly ground pepper to taste

4 hard-cooked eggs, shelled and quartered

6 anchovy fillets

2 tablespoons capers, rinsed and drained

COOK POTATOES in salted simmering water for 12 minutes. Drain and let cool. Cut into quarters. Cook beans in salted boiling water for 4 minutes. Drain and let cool. Cut into 2-inch pieces. **IN A LARGE BOWL,** combine potatoes, beans, pepper, tomatoes, onion, olives, and parsley. Break tuna into chunks and add to bowl. **IN A SMALL BOWL,** whisk oil, mustard, vinegar, garlic, salt, and pepper together. Pour half of dressing over tuna mixture. Toss gently and arrange on a large platter. Arrange egg wedges around edge of platter and garnish salad with anchovies and capers. Pass remaining dressing.

THREE-BEAN SALAD

Bean salads have been popular in this country since the Spaniards brought the first black beans, or "turtle" beans, from the Caribbean to Florida. Even then, a native American dish of cold cooked beans was already a widespread form of salad. The Florida custom of cooking black beans in rum assured their popularity there. Farther west, "Texas caviar" become fashionable, a Lone Star bean salad in which the cooked dried legumes marinate for a day or so in a spicy oil-and-vinegar dressing. In the Southwest, green chilies and cumin entered the picture. Beans on a bed of greens, known as ranch salad, was once all the rage in California. **Assembling** the dried beans for this dish is a little like playing with gemstones: the amber-brown borlotti, garnet cranberry beans, the soft jade of limas or favas. When the beans are cooked, their visual sparkle is translated into a wealth of flavors that make this a very unordinary three-bean salad.

^{1}/$_2$ cup dried cranberry beans

^{1}/$_2$ cup dried fava or lima beans

^{1}/$_2$ cup dried borlotti beans

1 cup yellow wax beans, trimmed, cut into 1-inch
   pieces

1 small red onion, chopped

1 cup pea shoots or bean sprouts

2 tablespoons cider vinegar

1 teaspoon honey

^{1}/$_4$ cup olive oil

Salt and freshly ground pepper to taste

3 fresh sage leaves, cut into strips

COOK CRANBERRY, fava or lima, and borlotti beans in simmering water until tender, about 45 minutes. Drain and let cool. Cook wax beans in salted boiling water for 3 minutes. Drain and let cool. **IN A LARGE BOWL,** combine beans with onion and pea shoots or sprouts. In a small bowl, whisk vinegar, honey, and oil together. Toss with bean mixture and add salt and pepper. Sprinkle with sage.

AMBROSIA

Everyone knows that ambrosia is the food of the gods, but lost in obscurity is the person who discovered that the gods liked marshmallows. And yet they must, since most traditional ambrosia recipes contain them, along with coconut, bananas, and oranges or, even more typical, canned mandarins. Purportedly a Southern dish often served at Christmas, the sticky-sweet combo was a staple of ladies' teas. In *Square Meals*, authors Jane and Michael Stern even transformed it into a cake, although in the process they had to omit the marshmallows. **We've followed** suit and introduced a few other updates that make this version—with toasted coconut, ricotta, and dried cranberries—a great brunch salad, side dish, or even a dessert.

1 cup ricotta cheese

1 cup plain yogurt

$1/4$ cup packed brown sugar

1 tablespoon fresh lemon juice

1 cup fresh pineapple chunks

2 tangerines, peeled and sectioned (see page 32)

1 cup red seedless grapes, halved

1 cup green seedless grapes halved

$1/2$ cup dried cranberries

1 cup shredded coconut, toasted (see page 32)

Fresh mint leaves for garnish

IN A BLENDER or food processor, purée cheese, yogurt, brown sugar, and lemon juice. Transfer to a large bowl. Stir in fruit and coconut. Refrigerate for about 2 hours, or until chilled. Serve garnished with mint leaves.

PARTY SALADS

05

DESIGNED TO DAZZLE, PARTY SALADS INCLUDE SPECTACULAR CROWD-PLEASERS AND FESTIVE HOLIDAY SPECIALS, AS WELL AS SALADS FOR SAMPLING AT A BUFFET. AND EACH HAS A LITTLE EXTRA FESTIVENESS AND SPARKLE THAT GIVES IT AN UNDENIABLE PARTY PERSONALITY.

YOU MAY CHOOSE TO SET OUT SEVERAL SIMULTANEOUSLY AS A KIND OF SALAD BUFFET, OR SERVE THEM IN COURSES AT THE DINNER TABLE, OR EVEN PUT OUT THE INGREDIENTS SO PEOPLE CAN COMPOSE THEIR OWN WITH THE RECIPE ON DISPLAY AS A GUIDE. IN ANY CASE, FOR MAXIMUM FLEXIBILITY, THESE SALADS HAVE A CERTAIN NONWILTABLE LONGEVITY, SO THEY CAN BE LEFT OUT FOR RELATIVELY LONG PERIODS. THIS ALSO MAKES THEM EXCELLENT POTLUCK CONTRIBUTIONS THE NEXT TIME SOMEONE ELSE IS DOING THE INVITING AND IT'S YOUR TURN TO BE THE PERFECT PARTY GUEST.

COUSCOUS, CRANBERRY, AND GARBANZO SALAD

Although the average person in this country consumes a pound of cranberries a year, hardly anyone ever eats a cranberry in its natural state. Until recently, virtually all this consumption was due to cranberry sauce, commercial or homemade. But the availability of the jewellike, dried version has given cranberries new popularity for reasons that are obvious in this cranberry-studded dish.

2 cups chicken stock

¹/₂ cup water

¹/₂ cup olive oil

¹/₄ teaspoon ground turmeric

¹/₄ teaspoon ground ginger

¹/₄ teaspoon ground cinnamon

2 cups instant couscous

1 cup dried cranberries

2 small zucchini, cut into ¹/₂-inch dice

2 carrots, peeled and cut into ¹/₂-inch dice

2 scallions, thinly sliced

15 ounces canned garbanzo beans, drained and rinsed

¹/₄ cup fresh lemon juice

¹/₂ teaspoon salt

¹/₈ teaspoon cayenne pepper

¹/₂ cup chopped fresh parsley

IN A LARGE SAUCEPAN, combine stock, water, ¹/₄ cup oil, turmeric, ginger, and cinnamon and bring to a boil. Gradually stir in couscous. Cook, stirring, until liquid is absorbed, about 3 minutes. Stir in the cranberries, cover, and let stand 15 minutes. Transfer to a large bowl and let cool to room temperature. Break up any couscous lumps with your fingers. Stir in zucchini, carrots, scallions, and garbanzos. **IN A SMALL BOWL,** whisk lemon juice, remaining ¹/₄ cup oil, salt, and cayenne together. Pour over couscous salad and toss well. Cover and refrigerate for at least 1 hour or as long as overnight. Just before serving, taste and adjust seasoning. Garnish with chopped parsley.

SANTA FE SHRIMP, CORN, AND BLACK BEAN SALAD

It's a small word, *toasted,* trailing behind the cumin seeds down there in the ingredient list. And you can, of course, ignore it. But once you taste this dressing in its unexpurgated toasted-seed version, you'll know we're not just nitpicking here. Either way though, the dressing underscores the lusty Southwestern character of this fiesta-time salad.

1¹/₂ cups dried black beans, soaked overnight

2 cups corn kernels (about 4 ears)

1 pound large shrimp, shelled

DRESSING:

1 tablespoon cumin seeds, toasted (see page 32)

¹/₄ cup red wine vinegar

2 tablespoons orange juice

2 teaspoons Dijon mustard

1 teaspoon honey

¹/₂ jalapeno chile, seeded and chopped

¹/₂ teaspoon salt

³/₄ cup olive oil

1 large red bell pepper, seeded, deribbed, and cut
   into thin strips

3 scallions, thinly sliced

1 cup fresh cilantro leaves

DRAIN BEANS and put in a large pot with cold water to cover. Simmer until beans are tender, about 45 minutes to 1 hour. (If the beans are old they will take longer.) Drain and let cool. **COOK CORN** in salted simmering water for 3 minutes. Drain and let cool. **COOK SHRIMP** in salted simmering water for 2 minutes, or until they turn bright pink. Drain and let cool. **TO MAKE DRESSING:** crush cumin seeds in a mortar. Whisk with remaining dressing ingredients until well blended. **IN LARGE BOWL,** toss beans, corn, bell pepper, scallions, and half of cilantro leaves with two thirds of dressing. In a medium bowl, toss shrimp with remaining dressing. Arrange shrimp over bean mixture and sprinkle with remaining cilantro leaves.

SPINACH SALAD SCHEHERAZADE

Although spinach salads have been rather popular of late, we discovered that adding spinach to salads is nothing new. John Evelyn, the seventeenth-century botanist and salad fan, however, wrote that when it came to spinach and salads, "the oftener [it is] kept out, the better." Tastes change, or maybe we have different varieties these days, but this salad, with its exotic touch of curried chutney dressing, always receives a warm welcome.

DRESSING:

3 tablespoons mango chutney

1/2 teaspoon curry powder

1 teaspoon Dijon mustard

1/4 cup balsamic vinegar

1 teaspoon honey

1/2 cup olive oil

Salt and freshly ground pepper to taste

8 cups (about 14 ounces) fresh spinach leaves, torn into bite-sized pieces

8 ounces smoked turkey or chicken, cut into strips

1/2 cup diced red onion

1 cup (5 ounces) cashews, toasted and coarsely chopped (see page 32)

IN A BLENDER or food processor, purée all dressing ingredients. In a large serving bowl, combine spinach, turkey or chicken, and onion. Toss with dressing and sprinkle with cashews.

CARROT COINS WITH TWO CORIANDERS

It's hard to believe that the aromatic coriander seed, with its tones of cumin, caraway, and lemon, is the source of the zesty little herb fresh coriander, also called cilantro, with its distinctive astringent zing. Yes, we know there are those who don't like cilantro at all, but for the rest of us, two corianders, as in this refreshing simple dish, are even better than one.

2 pounds carrots, peeled and cut into $1/8$-inch-
    thick slices
5 scallions, white part only, thinly sliced
1 cup fresh cilantro leaves

1 teaspoon ground cumin seed
1 teaspoon ground coriander
2 teaspoons honey
Salt and freshly ground pepper to taste

DRESSING:
5 tablespoons fresh lemon juice
2 tablespoons fresh orange juice
2 tablespoons white wine vinegar

IN A LARGE POT of boiling water, cook carrots for 2 minutes. Rinse under cold water to stop cooking, and drain. In a large bowl, combine carrots, scallions, and $3/4$ cup of cilantro. **IN A SMALL BOWL,** whisk all dressing ingredients together until smooth. Toss carrot mixture with dressing and sprinkle with remaining cilantro leaves.

CAPONATA IN CRISP ROMAINE LEAVES

Arab traders brought the eggplant to the Mediterranean in the Middle Ages, where it was greeted with an enthusiasm that led to everything from Greek moussaka to Turkish *imam bayeldi* to Italian caponata. Our version of the latter, presented on a large platter, makes a versatile party dish that can be served on individual plates or eaten as finger food.

Leaves from 2 heads fresh romaine lettuce

CAPONATA:

1/4 **cup olive oil**

1 globe eggplant, diced

1 onion, chopped

6 ripe Roma (plum) tomatoes, seeded and chopped (see page 133)

1 tablespoon tomato paste

1 tablespoon red wine vinegar

1/2 **cup imported black olives, pitted and halved**

2 tablespoons capers, drained and rinsed

Salt and freshly ground pepper to taste

1/2 **cup (2 ounces) walnuts, toasted and coarsely chopped (see page 32)**

1/2 **cup golden raisins, soaked in 3 tablespoons dry red wine for 1 hour**

1/2 **cup chopped fresh parsley**

CHOOSE ONLY the pale green smallish inner leaves of the romaine, reserving the other leaves for another use. Wrap in paper towels, place in a plastic bag, and refrigerate until ready to use. **TO MAKE CAPONATA:** In a large skillet over medium heat, heat oil and sauté eggplant and onion for about 5 minutes, or until barely tender. Add all remaining caponata ingredients except parsley and cook, uncovered, over medium heat for about 10 minutes. Stir every so often to prevent sticking. Let cool and taste for salt and pepper. Refrigerate in covered container until ready to use. **TO ASSEMBLE SALAD,** place romaine leaves in a spokelike fashion on a large round platter. Place about 2 table-spoons caponata on curly end of each leaf. Sprinkle with parsley.

COMPOSED SALAD OF SMOKED TROUT, CUCUMBER, AND RADISHES

serves 8

We love both the texture and flavor of smoked trout, which is why we don't understand the penchant for mashing it into mousses or whirling it inconsiderately into purées. Here, its complex delicacy comes through in a dish that makes a perfect spring brunch, a bridal shower centerpiece, or an excellent meal for anything extra special.

DRESSING:

6 tablespoons fresh lemon juice

2 teaspoons Dijon mustard

2 tablespoons crème fraîche or heavy cream

$1/2$ cup vegetable oil

$1^1/2$ teaspoons minced fresh tarragon leaves, or

$1/2$ teaspoon dried tarragon

Salt and freshly ground pepper to taste

1 pound smoked trout, skinned and boned

1 English (hothouse) cucumber, peeled, halved

lengthwise, and seeded

$1/4$ cup snipped fresh dill

2 cups red radishes

1 cup white radishes

3 bunches watercress, stemmed

$1/2$ cup plus 2 tablespoons snipped fresh chives

IN A SMALL BOWL, whisk together all dressing ingredients until well blended. Cut trout into strips and put in a medium bowl. Slice cucumber very thin and add to bowl with half of dill. Toss with half of dressing. **SLICE RADISHES** very thin and put in a bowl with watercress and $1/2$ cup chives. Toss with remaining dressing. On large serving platter, make a bed of watercress mixture. Mound trout mixture on top. Sprinkle with remaining dill and 2 tablespoons chives.

AUTUMN SALAD OF TURKEY, YAMS, AND GREEN BEANS

Serves 8 to 10

No law says this flavorful combination must be made with leftovers, but it's a good dish to keep in mind should you find a half-devoured roast turkey loitering in your refrigerator. With its clean crunch of peppers, mustardy tang, and the musty sweetness of yams, it's a welcome, fresh-tasting change from the usual post-holiday solutions.

2 yams or sweet potatoes, peeled and diced

1 pound green beans, cut into 2-inch pieces

4 cups diced cooked turkey

1 large red bell pepper, seeded, deribbed, and cut into strips

Leaves from 1 large head curly endive, torn into bite-sized pieces

DRESSING:

2 tablespoons minced shallots

1 1/2 teaspoons minced fresh rosemary, or 1/2 teaspoon dried rosemary

1 tablespoon hot-sweet mustard

1/4 cup red wine vinegar

1/2 cup olive oil

Salt and freshly ground pepper to taste

COOK YAMS in salted simmering water until tender, about 15 minutes. Drain and let cool. Cook green beans in salted simmering water until crisp-tender, about 4 minutes. Drain under cold water. Let cool. **IN A LARGE SERVING BOWL,** combine turkey, yams, green beans, bell pepper, and curly endive. In a small bowl, whisk all dressing ingredients together until well blended. Taste and adjust seasoning. Toss salad with dressing.

"HEART"ICHOKE
AND MUSHROOM SALAD

Eaten in the traditional manner, leaf by leaf, artichokes are the vegetable model of delayed gratification. We prefer to get right to the "heart" of the matter, the succulent center of attention in this luscious, mushroom-rich dish. This sensuous combination is a good dish for Valentine's Day, not an occasion for delayed gratification.

3 tablespoons fresh lemon juice

10 baby artichokes

$1/2$ cup dry white wine

$1/2$ cup olive oil

$3/4$ cup chicken stock or water

4 cloves garlic, halved

3 tablespoons chopped fresh parsley

2 tablespoons chopped fresh mint, plus fresh mint
   leaves for garnish

1 teaspoon coriander seeds, lightly crushed

$1/4$ teaspoon black peppercorns, coarsely ground

1 pound small white or brown mushrooms,
   quartered

Salt and freshly ground pepper to taste

FILL A LARGE BOWL with water and stir in lemon juice. Cut off stem and about $1/2$ inch from tip of each artichoke. Peel away about 2 layers of leaves until artichokes are pale green. Cut artichokes into quarters lengthwise and add artichokes to bowl of lemon water to prevent discoloration. **IN A LARGE SAUCEPAN,** combine wine, olive oil, stock or water, garlic, parsley, chopped mint, coriander, and peppercorns and bring to a boil. Drain artichokes, add to pan, cover, and simmer for 15 minutes. Add mushrooms and simmer another 10 minutes. Let cool and add salt and pepper. Put in a shallow bowl and sprinkle with mint leaves. Serve at room temperature.

SALAD OF PEARLS AND JADE

Not just another pretty pasta! That's the usual reaction to this mélange of petite ingredients that make for a big-tasting dish. Israeli couscous adds new interest to any pasta salad, but if you can't find it easily, try orzo or any other small pasta.

2 cups Israeli couscous (pearl pasta)

2 cups frozen petite peas

2 cups bay shrimp

1 cup pea shoots or bean sprouts

GINGER DRESSING:

2 tablespoons grated fresh ginger

1 teaspoon packed brown sugar

1 clove garlic, minced

$1/8$ teaspoon red pepper flakes

$1/4$ cup fresh lime juice

1 tablespoon Asian sesame oil

$1/2$ cup peanut or canola oil

Salt and freshly ground pepper to taste

Red lettuce leaves for serving

2 tablespoons sesame seeds, toasted (see page 32)

COOK COUSCOUS in a medium pot of salted boiling water for 8 to 9 minutes. Drain and let cool. Cook peas in salted boiling water for 4 minutes. Drain under cold water and cool. In a large bowl, combine pasta, peas, shrimp, and shoots or sprouts. **IN A BLENDER** or food processor, purée all dressing ingredients until smooth. Taste and adjust seasoning. Toss with couscous mixture. Line a serving plate with lettuce leaves and mound salad over them. Sprinkle with sesame seeds.

SWEET-HOT
ROASTED VEGETABLE SALAD

Although we don't detect much difference in taste between the slender, long Asian eggplants and their more common squat counterparts, in this dish the shape is the thing. Not only are the Asian varieties easier to handle and quicker to cook, the silky roasted slices add a sultry note to this tantalizing combination.

3 Asian eggplants, halved lengthwise

2 red bell peppers, quartered, seeded, and deribbed

2 large sweet onions, quartered

4 carrots, peeled

3 zucchini

1 head garlic, cloves separated

1 unpeeled large sweet potato, cut into $1/2$-inch slices

20 cherry tomatoes

$1/2$ cup olive oil

1 tablespoon ground cumin

1 tablespoon ground coriander

1 tablespoon fennel seeds

1 teaspoon red pepper flakes

$1/2$ cup balsamic vinegar

2 tablespoons low-salt soy sauce

1 tablespoon packed brown sugar

$1/2$ cup chopped fresh cilantro leaves

PREHEAT OVEN to 400°F. Brush all vegetables with oil and place all except tomatoes on a sided baking sheet. Combine cumin, coriander, fennel seeds, and pepper flakes and sprinkle over vegetables. **ROAST** for 30 minutes, then add tomatoes. Continue roasting another 15 minutes. Remove vegetables from baking sheet and pour juices into a saucepan. Add vinegar, soy sauce, and brown sugar and bring to a boil. Pour over vegetables and let marinate a few hours or overnight. Arrange vegetables on serving platter and sprinkle with chopped cilantro.

WHITE BEAN, FENNEL,
AND BLACK OLIVE SALAD

It may look like celery and taste a bit like licorice, but fennel isn't like anything else. Sliced thin and served raw, everything's good about it: its crunch, its spicy aroma, its satisfying sweetness. Mixed with creamy fat beans and briny olives, fennel only gets better, especially under the influence of good olive oil.

2 cups dried white beans (navy or cannellini),
    soaked in cold water overnight

1 large fennel bulb, trimmed, quartered, and thinly
    sliced

1 small red onion, diced

1/4 cup snipped fresh dill

DRESSING:

2 cloves garlic, crushed

1/2 teaspoon ground sage

2 tablespoons fresh lemon juice

3 tablespoon white wine vinegar

1/2 cup olive oil

Salt and freshly ground pepper to taste

1/2 cup imported black olives, pitted and halved

DRAIN BEANS and put in a large pot with cold water to cover. Simmer, partially covered, until tender, about 45 minutes. Drain and let cool. **IN A LARGE BOWL,** combine beans, fennel, onion, and dill. In a small bowl, whisk all dressing ingredients together until well blended. Taste and adjust seasoning. Toss with bean mixture. Sprinkle with olives and serve at room temperature.

WINTER CHICKEN SALAD WITH BROCCOLI AND TOASTED WALNUTS

Serves 8

Chunks of chicken and toasted walnuts make this broccoli-based salad a substantial dish, hearty enough to satisfy a gathering of television football fans on a cold winter's day. Tarragon and lemon add a subtle delicacy that is more easily noticed on less grueling occasions.

3 skinless, boneless whole chicken breasts

1 bunch broccoli, trimmed and cut into 1-inch pieces

1 cup (4 ounces) walnuts, toasted and coarsely chopped (see page 32)

1 1/2 teaspoons minced fresh tarragon, or 1/2 teaspoon dried tarragon

2 tablespoons fresh lemon juice

1/2 cup mayonnaise

1/4 cup plain yogurt or sour cream

1/8 teaspoon cayenne pepper

Salt and freshly ground pepper to taste

2 cups mixed salad greens

PUT CHICKEN in a large skillet and cover with cold water. Add salt and pepper. Simmer for 8 minutes, cover, and remove from heat. Let chicken rest in pan until cool enough to handle. **COOK BROCCOLI** in salted boiling water until crisp-tender, about 6 minutes. Drain under cold water and let cool. **CUT CHICKEN** into 1/2-inch cubes and broccoli into bite-sized pieces. In a large bowl, combine chicken, broccoli, 3/4 cup walnuts, and half of tarragon. **IN A SMALL BOWL,** mix remaining tarragon, lemon juice, mayonnaise, yogurt or sour cream, cayenne, salt, and pepper until blended. Toss with chicken mixture. Taste and adjust seasoning. **LINE A SERVING** dish with salad greens. Mound chicken mixture over them. Sprinkle with remaining walnuts.

GRILLED SUMMER CHICKEN SALAD WITH NEW POTATOES, GREEN BEANS, AND TOMATOES

There's no doubt that juicy strips of golden brown grilled chicken make this dish irresistible, but it's the cherry tomatoes that make it glitter. Any farmer's market and many supermarkets will give you choices of cherry tomatoes, from tiny persimmon-colored "currant" tomatoes to yellow and red pear-shaped miniatures, as well as Tiny Tims, Golden Pygmies, and flavorful, multicolored Pixies. We make this easy dish often during the summer, and the variety of tomatoes makes it a little different every time.

2 pounds small red potatoes

1 pound green beans, cut into 2-inch pieces

1 cup olive oil

6 tablespoons fresh lemon juice

6 boneless, skinless chicken breast halves

1 teaspoon salt

3 tablespoons chopped fresh basil

1 teaspoon minced fresh thyme, or $\frac{1}{2}$ teaspoon dried thyme

1 clove garlic, crushed

$\frac{1}{2}$ teaspoon ground pepper

1 tablespoon Dijon mustard

1 cup red cherry tomatoes, halved

1 cup yellow cherry tomatoes, halved

1 red bell pepper, seeded, deribbed, and cut into strips

1 cup niçoise olives, pitted and halved

3 tablespoons capers, drained and rinsed

3 cups arugula leaves

Salt to taste

COOK POTATOES in salted boiling water until tender, about 12 minutes. Drain, let cool, and cut into quarters. Cook beans in salted boiling water until crisp-tender, about 3 minutes. Drain under cold water and let cool. **LIGHT A FIRE** in a charcoal grill or preheat a gas grill or broiler. In a small bowl, whisk half of oil and half of lemon juice together. Brush chicken on both sides with this mixture and sprinkle with salt. Grill or broil chicken for about 4 minutes on each side. Let cool and cut into $\frac{1}{2}$-inch strips. **WHISK** remaining oil, remaining lemon juice, basil, thyme, garlic, pepper, and mustard together. Put chicken strips in a large bowl and combine with potatoes, green beans, tomatoes, bell pepper, olives, capers, and arugula. Toss with dressing and add salt.

CHERRY TOMATO
AND RICOTTA SALATA SALAD

Like balsamic vinegar and arugula, ricotta salata cheese is one of those "new" ingredients that food-wise Italy has been quietly enjoying for quite awhile. Its dry texture and salty taste (hence *salata*) contrast here with the summer sugar of tomatoes and the spice of arugula.

½ cup extra-virgin olive oil

¼ cup best-quality balsamic vinegar

2 cups red cherry tomatoes, halved

2 cups yellow cherry tomatoes, halved

6 cups arugula (about 8 ounces)

Salt and freshly ground pepper to taste

6 ounces ricotta salata cheese

1 cup fresh basil leaves

IN A SMALL BOWL, whisk oil and vinegar together. In a large bowl, gently combine tomatoes and arugula. Toss with dressing and place in a shallow serving bowl. Add salt and pepper. Shave thin slices of ricotta salata and place over tomato mixture. Sprinkle with basil.

NOTES

PICNIC
SALADS

POTATO SALADS, SLAWS, TAILGATE SALADS, GRILLED SALADS, BARBECUED BEANS—ALL PORTABLE, APPETIZING, AND IMPERVIOUS TO LONG AFTERNOONS ON A PICNIC TABLE. HERE ARE UPDATED CLASSICS, KID-FRIENDLY COMBOS, AND CONTEMPORARY, ALMOST-TRENDY MÉLANGES. IN THE BEGINNING, AS ANY PICNIC-LOVER KNOWS, IS THE POTATO.

THE MIGHTY POTATO SALAD:
FIVE VARIATIONS ON A BELOVED THEME

To many people, a salad that contains even one small potato is, quite simply, potato salad. To determine more about a salad's ethnic identity, we must look at its accompanying ingredients. With mayonnaise or salad dressing, in both hot and cold versions, the potato salad is associated with German Americans, who all but invented the dish in this country. Needless to say, the Irish have also contributed their fair share of potato salads, ever since Irish Presbyterians planted their first crop of the white tubers in Londonderry, New Hampshire, in the 1720s. Cold potatoes with aioli have French-Italian roots, and those in saffron or peppery dressings are usually Hispanic. **Whatever** its culinary roots, the potato salad has been ordained by food historian Evan Jones as the most American of all vegetable salads. In any version, potato salads are testimony to the home cook's respect for and genius with simple, natural ingredients. And, of course, as picnic fare, they are as indispensable as ants.

HERBED POTATO SALAD WITH CRISPY BACON AND SWEET PEAS

A scattering of peas brings a touch of green and a lively burst of sweetness to this picnic favorite enlivened with fresh herbs and the savory crunch of bacon.

DRESSING:

1/4 cup minced shallots

2 tablespoons snipped fresh dill

1 tablespoon minced fresh tarragon

3 tablespoons chopped fresh parsley

2 cloves garlic, minced

3 tablespoons Dijon mustard

5 tablespoons white wine vinegar

3/4 cup olive oil

Salt and freshly ground pepper to taste

3 pounds small red potatoes

4 cups fresh or frozen peas

8 ounces sliced bacon, cooked until crisp and
crumbled

IN A SMALL BOWL, whisk all dressing ingredients together until well blended. Set aside. Cook potatoes in boiling salted water for about 12 minutes. Drain, let cool to touch, and cut into quarters. Cook fresh peas in salted boiling water for 6 minutes, frozen peas for 3 minutes. Drain under cold water and let cool. **IN A LARGE BOWL,** toss still-warm potatoes with about half of dressing and let cool. Combine with peas and bacon and add remaining dressing. Taste and adjust seasoning.

ONE POTATO, TWO POTATO

This pretty combo brings warm autumn colors to the picnic table any time of the year.

DRESSING:

¹/₄ cup minced shallots

2 tablespoons grainy mustard

2 tablespoons honey mustard

1¹/₂ teaspoons minced fresh tarragon leaves or

  ¹/₂ teaspoon dried tarragon

¹/₄ cup red wine vinegar

¹/₂ cup olive oil

1¹/₂ pounds boiling potatoes, peeled and cut into

  ³/₄-inch cubes

1¹/₂ pounds sweet potatoes (or yams), peeled and

  cut into ³/₄-inch cubes

1 pound green beans, cut into ¹/₂-inch pieces

1 small red onion, diced

¹/₂ cup snipped fresh chives

Salt and freshly ground pepper to taste

IN A BLENDER or food processor, process all dressing ingredients until thick and fairly smooth. Cook boiling potatoes and sweet potatoes or yams in salted boiling water until tender, about 11 minutes. Drain and let cool. Cook green beans in salted boiling water until crisp-tender, about 4 minutes. Drain under cold water. **IN A LARGE BOWL,** combine potatoes, green beans, red onion, and chives. Toss with dressing. Add salt and pepper.

OLD-FASHIONED POTATO SALAD

serves 8 to 10

No one ever tires of this velvety classic with its irresistible lure of crumbled bacon.

2 pounds boiling potatoes, peeled and sliced

6 slices bacon

2 tablespoons sugar

1 teaspoon flour

$1/2$ teaspoon salt

$1/4$ teaspoon ground pepper

$1/4$ cup red wine vinegar

$1/2$ cup water

1 onion, chopped

3 celery stalks, sliced

2 hard-cooked eggs, sliced

1 tablespoon snipped fresh dill

COOK POTATOES in salted boiling water until tender, about 15 minutes. In a large skillet, cook bacon until crisp. With a slotted metal spatula, transfer bacon to paper towels to drain. Crumble bacon. DRAIN PAN of all but 2 tablespoons drippings. Add sugar, flour, salt, and pepper and stir until smooth. Stir in vinegar and water and bring to a boil. Add onion and mix well. In a large bowl, combine potatoes, celery, and eggs. Toss with dressing and top with bacon and dill.

NEW-FASHIONED POTATO SALAD

Even the most discriminating picnickers welcome this wine-accented mixture, rich with slivers of fennel, sun-dried tomatoes, and fat, oily olives.

DRESSING:

$^1/_2$ cup dry white wine

1 tablespoon champagne vinegar

$^1/_2$ teaspoon salt

$^1/_4$ teaspoon ground pepper

1 tablespoon Dijon mustard

1$^1/_2$ teaspoons minced fresh rosemary, or
   $^1/_2$ teaspoon dried rosemary

$^1/_2$ cup olive oil

2 pounds small red potatoes

$^1/_2$ cup oil-packed sun-dried tomatoes, drained and
   cut into thin strips

$^1/_2$ cup imported black olives, pitted and halved

1 small fennel bulb, trimmed, cored, and cut into
   thin strips

3 scallions, thinly sliced

1 fresh rosemary sprig for garnish

IN A SMALL BOWL, whisk all dressing ingredients together. Cook potatoes in salted boiling water until tender, about 12 minutes. Let cool and slice $^1/_4$ inch thick. **IN A LARGE BOWL,** combine potatoes, tomatoes, olives, fennel, and scallions. Toss with dressing. Taste and adjust seasoning. Garnish with rosemary sprig.

POTATO, WATERCRESS, AND BLUE CHEESE SALAD

serves > 6 to 8

Even if you're not in a hurry, you don't have to bother peeling these pale pink spuds—their skins add both texture and flavor.

2 pounds unpeeled small red potatoes

DRESSING:

$^1/_4$ **cup watercress leaves**

$^1/_4$ **cup white wine vinegar**

2 tablespoons Dijon mustard

$^1/_4$ **teaspoon salt**

$^1/_4$ **teaspoon ground pepper**

$^1/_2$ **cup olive oil**

4 celery stalks, thinly sliced

2 cups watercress leaves

$1^3/_4$ **cups (8 ounces) blue cheese, crumbled**

COOK POTATOES in salted boiling water until tender, about 12 minutes. Let cool and cut into quarters. In a blender or food processor, process all dressing ingredients until smooth. **IN A LARGE BOWL,** combine potatoes, celery, watercress, and half of blue cheese. Toss with dressing and top with remaining cheese.

PENNE SALAD PROVENÇAL

Anyone who has ordered veal piccata knows the moment of hope that this time, maybe, there will be enough capers in the sauce. But like most caper-containing dishes, it usually arrives with a minor sprinkling of the pungent little pearls, just enough to refresh the memory about how good capers are and how much better more would be. **This miserly** allocation stems from concerns more economic than gastronomic: Capers are expensive. This is because the viney caper plant, which grows wild in poor soil and rock piles, requires close attention and hand tending to catch the buds just before they bloom. Although the flowers are beautiful—lush white petals with bright violet stamens—to caper fans, every bloom is a morsel lost. (On the other hand, Nora Ephron in her book *Heartburn* insists, "Nobody really likes capers, no matter what you do with them.") **Caper addicts** love this richly delicious pasta salad in which capers abound—though it is always possible to sneak in a few more.

1 pound penne pasta

8 ounces green beans, cut into 1-inch pieces

1 small red onion, cut into 1/4-inch dice

1 small zucchini, cut into 1/4-inch dice

1 red bell pepper, seeded, deribbed and cut into
    1/4-inch dice

1 large ripe tomato, seeded and diced (see note)

1 cup niçoise olives, pitted and halved

1/4 cup capers, drained and rinsed

BASIL VINAIGRETTE:

1 cup fresh basil leaves

1/2 cup olive oil

1/4 cup white wine vinegar

2 cloves garlic, minced

Salt and freshly ground pepper to taste

COOK PENNE according to package directions. Drain and let cool. Cook green beans in salted, boiling water until crisp-tender, about 4 minutes. Drain under cold water and let cool. **IN A LARGE BOWL,** combine penne, green beans, onion, zucchini, pepper, tomato, olives, and capers. In a food processor or blender, process all vinaigrette ingredients until smooth. Pour over pasta and toss well. Taste for salt and pepper. Let salad sit for about 2 hours at room temperature before serving. Taste and adjust seasoning if necessary.

SEEDING TOMATOES: Cut tomatoes in half and squeeze seeds from each half.

FLAGEOLET, CORN, AND FENNEL SALAD

Though small in size, the flageolet has perhaps the best flavor of all dried beans. Its delicate celadon color and French connections also give it a certain panache, yet it is simply a kidney bean in its immature state. Combined with the sunny glints of papaya and corn, flageolets make an unusual salad, radiant with exquisite colors.

1 cup dried flageolet beans, soaked in cold water overnight

2 cups corn kernels (about 4 ears)

1 large fennel bulb, trimmed and cut into $1/2$-inch dice

1 small red onion, cut into $1/2$-inch dice

1 small papaya, seeded, peeled, and diced

$1/4$ cup fresh mint leaves, coarsely chopped

$1/4$ cup fresh parsley leaves, chopped

CUMIN VINAIGRETTE:

2 tablespoons fresh lime juice

2 tablespoons sherry vinegar

1 teaspoon ground cumin

6 tablespoons olive oil

Salt and freshly ground pepper to taste

Fresh mint leaves for garnish

DRAIN BEANS and put in pot with cold water to cover. Bring to a boil, partially cover, reduce heat, and simmer 35 to 45 minutes or until tender. Drain and let cool. **COOK CORN** in salted boiling water until tender, about 3 minutes. Let cool. In a large bowl, combine beans, corn, fennel, onion, papaya, mint, and parsley. In a small bowl, whisk all vinaigrette ingredients together. Toss with bean mixture. Garnish with mint.

ROSY RICE SALAD

serves > 8

The first rice salad probably originated on the day after a big party, when the larder bulged with small containers of leftovers. Because rice comes in no less than eight thousand varieties, there is bound to be at least one that will complement and enhance any mix of ingredients. Our choice here is the exotic jasmine, a tender, long-grained Thai rice that helps this rose-tinged salad taste as bright as it looks.

1½ cups jasmine rice

2 beets, roasted, peeled, and diced (see page 63)

1 English (hothouse) cucumber, peeled, seeded,
   and diced

6 red radishes, diced

½ cup snipped fresh chives

½ cup toasted pine nuts (see page 32)

½ cup golden raisins

DRESSING:

¼ cup balsamic vinegar

⅓ cup olive oil

1 teaspoon hot-sweet mustard

Salt and freshly ground pepper to taste

RINSE RICE in a strainer until water runs clear. Cook rice in a covered saucepan of 3½ cups salted simmering water for 18 minutes. Remove from heat, fluff with a fork, and let sit, covered with a tea towel, for 5 minutes. Let cool. **IN A LARGE BOWL,** combine rice, beets, cucumber, radishes, chives, pine nuts, and raisins. In a small bowl, whisk all dressing ingredients together. Toss with rice mixture and taste for salt and pepper.

CREAMY CURRY SLAW

We get the word *coleslaw* from the Dutch, whose great "cabbage salads" spread from their East Coast settlements in eighteenth-century New Netherland to general popularity throughout the country. However, the Dutch would probably never recognize this spicy translation of their beloved *koolslaa,* with its lively accents of cilantro and curry.

DRESSING:

1 clove garlic, minced

1 cup plain yogurt

2 tablespoons sugar

2 tablespoons cider vinegar

1 tablespoon fresh lime or lemon juice

1 teaspoon curry powder, or to taste

1 large (about 2$\frac{1}{2}$ pounds) cabbage, cored and shredded

4 carrots, peeled and grated

2 cups golden raisins

1 bunch scallions, thinly sliced

$\frac{1}{2}$ cup coarsely chopped fresh cilantro

$\frac{1}{2}$ cup chopped fresh parsley

IN A SMALL BOWL, whisk all dressing ingredients together. In a large bowl, combine cabbage, carrots, raisins, scallions, half of cilantro, and half of parsley. Toss with dressing. Taste and adjust seasoning. Sprinkle with remaining cilantro and parsley.

PEPPER AND PINEAPPLE SLAW

Sweet heat is just the first sensation in this tropics-inspired dish, which also happens to be lovely to look at. The mix of fresh fruit and shredded vegetables gives this unconventional slaw a range of alluring qualities, from succulent to crunchy, juicy to crisp.

DRESSING:

1 jalapeño chile, seeded and minced

2 tablespoons honey

1 teaspoon ground cumin

$1/4$ cup fresh lime juice

$1/4$ cup fresh lemon juice

$1/2$ cup vegetable or corn oil

$1/2$ teaspoon salt

1 napa cabbage, cored and shredded

1 red bell pepper, seeded, deribbed and cut into
   strips

1 small fresh pineapple, peeled, cored, and diced
   (about 3 cups)

1 small jicama, peeled and cut into matchsticks
   (about 2 cups)

$1/2$ cup chopped fresh cilantro

IN A SMALL BOWL, whisk all dressing ingredients together. In a large bowl, combine cabbage with all remaining ingredients. Toss with dressing. Taste and adjust seasoning.

BARBECUED BEAN SALAD

The New World word *barbecue* was first used to refer to the cooking methods of the Haitian Indians, who cooked their food on outdoor grills, or *barbacoas.* The Spanish adopted the custom but heightened flavors with sauces and marinades. This is the heritage of barbecued beans, a traditional Southern way with all kinds of beans from baby limas to green beans. For an old-fashioned all-American picnic, these barbecued beans couldn't be more authentic.

BARBECUE SAUCE VINAIGRETTE:

1/4 cup tomato-based barbecue sauce

1 teaspoon Dijon mustard

2 tablespoons balsamic vinegar

1/2 cup corn oil

1/2 teaspoon dried sage, crumbled

8 ounces yellow wax beans, cut into 2 inch pieces

2 cups cooked pinto beans, drained

2 cups cooked cannellini beans, drained

2 cups cooked baby lima beans, drained

2 cups shredded iceberg lettuce

COOK WAX BEANS in salted boiling water until crisp-tender. Drain under cold water and let cool. **IN A SMALL BOWL,** whisk all vinaigrette ingredients together. In a large bowl, combine all beans with lettuce. Toss with vinaigrette.

SWEET AND HOT RED PEPPER SALAD

serves > 6 to 8

A ramble through any farmers' market offers a panoply of peppers. Though they come in a mind-boggling array of shapes, colors, and sizes, they are basically either sweet or hot. Color selection includes purple, green, chocolate-brown, and even white, but for visual appeal, strips of fire-engine red ones are our choice here. A sprinkle of cayenne adds a touch of real fire.

2 pounds red bell peppers, roasted, peeled, and
   seeded (see page 32)
2 tablespoons olive oil
1 tablespoon balsamic vinegar
1 tablespoon fresh lemon juice
1 tablespoon honey
$1/2$ teaspoon ground cumin
Pinch of cayenne pepper
2 cloves garlic, minced
Salt and freshly ground pepper to taste
Chopped fresh parsley for garnish

CUT RED PEPPERS into strips and put in a shallow bowl. Combine all the remaining ingredients except parsley and toss with peppers. Let marinate a few hours or overnight. Sprinkle with parsley.

HONEYED CARROT SALAD WITH CUMIN

If you're a "What can I bring to the picnic?" kind of person, this is the salad to remember. You can make it at the last minute or a day ahead, it takes no time to put together, and its honey-spice flavors are downright exciting. Nonwiltable, sturdy, and portable, it is especially suitable for picnics.

2 pounds carrots, peeled and thinly sliced

$^{1}/_{4}$ teaspoon ground cinnamon

$^{1}/_{8}$ teaspoon cayenne pepper

1 tablespoon ground cumin

$^{1}/_{2}$ cup fresh lemon juice

2 tablespoons honey

2 tablespoons chopped fresh parsley

2 tablespoons chopped fresh cilantro

3 tablespoons olive oil

Salt and freshly ground pepper to taste

COOK CARROTS in salted boiling water just until tender, about 4 minutes. Drain and put in a large bowl. In a small bowl, whisk all remaining ingredients together and toss with carrots. Taste and adjust seasoning. Serve cold or at room temperature.

TWO-PEA AND SPINACH SALAD

Split peas are simply fresh peas that have been dried, a process that splits them in half. As soup and "pease porridge," split peas have been historically consumed in larger quantities than the fresh vegetable, partly because their almost eternal life keeps them constantly available. By contrast, fresh peas give us, in each nuggety bite, the ephemeral intensity of summer. Add a scattering of baby spinach leaves, and you have a salad that offers the best of both worlds.

1 pound yellow split peas

2 cloves garlic, minced

$1/2$ teaspoon salt

2 pounds fresh peas, shelled (about 2 cups)

$1/2$ red onion, diced

4 cups baby spinach leaves, coarsely chopped

3 tablespoons sherry vinegar

$1/3$ cup olive oil

Salt and freshly ground pepper to taste

PICK OVER and rinse split peas. Cook in salted simmering water with garlic for about 25 minutes, or until just tender. Add fresh peas and cook another 3 minutes. Drain and let cool. **PUT PEAS** in a large bowl and add onion and spinach. In a small bowl, whisk vinegar and oil together and toss with pea mixture. Add salt and pepper.

SUCCOTASH SALAD

While fresh fava beans have a definite cachet these days, the old reliable lima seems a bit mundane. This may be a holdover from its association with succotash, which too many people remember from their grammar school hot-lunch programs—or tepid-lunch programs, as the case may be. Yet the bean-corn combination has a venerable past, beginning with the Native Americans who taught the settlers the art of "msickquatash." They even froze it in blocks and chopped off a chunk whenever a craving for succotash became too strong to resist. The Pennsylvania Dutch made it into a kind of stew, adding peppers, tomatoes, and onions. New Englanders stripped just-picked corn from the cob for their beloved version. Before the canning industry divested the dish of its intrinsic and varied character, people loved succotash. Food historian Evan Jones reports a Vermont farmer whose entries included nothing at all about food except one event the middle of August 1898: "This day," he wrote, "I din'd upon Succotash." In this salad, the buttery limas contrast with the tartness of lemon and buttermilk—succotash is back!

2 cups fresh corn kernels (about 4 ears)

2 cups frozen baby lima beans

2 cups peas

BUTTERMILK DRESSING:

1/2 cup buttermilk

2 tablespoons mayonnaise

1 tablespoon fresh lemon juice

1/4 teaspoon red pepper flakes

3 tablespoon chopped fresh parsley

1/2 cup chopped scallions

Salt and freshly ground pepper to taste

COOK CORN, lima beans, and peas in salted boiling water for 3 minutes. Drain under cold water and cool. In a small bowl, whisk all dressing ingredients together. In a large bowl, combine corn, lima beans, peas, and scallions. Toss with dressing. Season with salt and pepper. Refrigerate until ready to serve.

COLESLAW WITH
SWEET AND SOUR VINAIGRETTE

As a method of preserving food, the making of pickles and relishes has always been popular with American cooks, possibly because of our native penchant for any extra touch of sweetness. Pickles were made from anything—from peaches to nasturtium seeds—and their variety lent color and pungency all through the winter. Derived from a Middle English word meaning a "taste," relish has been part of the our culinary language for about two hundred years. Taste is what this sweet pickle relish, whisked up with a little rice wine vinegar, adds to these colorfully intertwined shreds of cabbage and carrot.

SWEET AND SOUR VINAIGRETTE:

1 tablespoon honey

3 tablespoons rice vinegar

3 tablespoons vegetable oil

1 tablespoon minced fresh dill

1/4 cup sweet pickle relish

1/2 red cabbage, cored and shredded

1/2 savoy or green cabbage, cored and shredded

2 carrots, shredded

1 yellow or red bell pepper, seeded, deribbed and
    cut into thin strips

Salt and freshly ground pepper to taste

IN A MEDIUM BOWL, whisk honey, vinegar, and oil together. Stir in dill and relish. In a large bowl, combine cabbages, carrots, and bell peppers. Toss with vinaigrette. Add salt and pepper.

RED AND BLACK LENTIL SALAD
WITH CAPERS

Because of their growing popularity, lentils are available in more colors, sizes, and types than ever before. There are hardy brown ones, sometimes called German, and the delicate, blue-green French *lentilles de Puy.* Here we've used black lentils and the salmon-orange variety sold in specialty shops as Egyptian lentils, *masoor dal,* or red lentils, some of which may turn golden yellow when cooked. For this salad, the reds and blacks are cooked separately because the latter takes twice as long to cook as the former, which can fall apart if cooked even a minute too long. **Lentil connoisseurs,** a growing breed, insist that there are important subtle differences among all lentils. However Jane Grigson, in her *Vegetable Book,* proposes that "few people at a blind tasting could tell the difference."

1 cup red lentils

1 cup black lentils

2 carrots, peeled and finely grated

$\frac{1}{2}$ cup chopped fresh parsley

$\frac{1}{4}$ cup capers, drained, rinsed, and coarsely
   chopped

VINAIGRETTE:

3 tablespoons red wine vinegar

1 teaspoon Dijon mustard

1 clove garlic, minced

$\frac{1}{2}$ cup olive oil

2 tablespoons snipped fresh chives

$1\frac{1}{2}$ teaspoons minced fresh tarragon, or $\frac{1}{2}$ teaspoon
   dried tarragon

Salt and freshly ground pepper to taste

PICK OVER and rinse lentils. Cook red lentils, covered, in 3 cups salted simmering water for about 13 minutes, or until just tender. Drain and let cool. Cook black lentils, covered, in 3 cups salted simmering water for about 25 minutes, or until just tender. Drain and let cool. **IN A LARGE BOWL,** combine lentils, carrots, parsley, and capers. **TO MAKE VINAIGRETTE:** In a medium bowl, whisk vinegar, mustard, garlic, and oil together. Stir in chives, tarragon, salt, and pepper. Add to lentils and toss well to combine. Taste and adjust seasoning.

CRISP CARROT AND ZUCCHINI SALAD WITH CURRANTS

serves > 6

Across a crowded picnic table, this modest-looking mélange of carrot and zucchini matchsticks may not seem too enchanting, but it has invisible charms. Macerated in raspberry vinegar, the currants give each forkful a burst of fruity flavor. (Resist the temptation to substitute raisins—it's worth a trip to the store, really.) Zucchini's soakablity is put to use here as a splash of walnut oil intensifies its natural, mild nuttiness. An easy dish, and according to many a delighted guest, a diamond in the rough.

$1/2$ **cup dried currants soaked in** $1/4$ **cup raspberry vinegar for 1 hour**

3 large carrots, peeled and cut into matchsticks

3 zucchini, cut into matchsticks

Salt and freshly ground pepper to taste

$1/4$ **cup snipped fresh chives for garnish**

DRESSING:

2 tablespoons walnut oil

3 tablespoons olive oil

$1/2$ **teaspoon dried oregano**

$1/2$ **teaspoon dried thyme**

DRAIN currants and reserve vinegar for dressing. Cook carrots and zucchini in salted boiling water for 2 minutes, or until just tender. Drain and place in a large bowl with currants. **IN A MEDIUM BOWL,** mix reserved vinegar with oils, oregano, and thyme. Pour over still-warm carrots and zucchini and toss well. Let cool and add salt and pepper. Garnish with chives and serve.

MODERN MACARONI SALAD

Not your mama's macaroni salad this, with its goat cheese and sun-dried tomatoes, watercress and hot-sweet mustard; but it has the appeal that has made the classic dish a longtime favorite. Though its exact origins are unknown, no less a personage than Thomas Jefferson ordered "a stock of Maccaroni" along with several other salad ingredients including mustard, anchovies, Parmesan cheese, oil, and even "Vinaigre d'Estragon." He was also the first American to place an order for a "macaroni machine," though food historians assure us that the English had already brought maca-roni to these shores. By the 1890s this country's food producers had contributed their truly American touch, as canned macaroni became readily available. In this salad, almost anything else will work beautifully.

1 pound macaroni

2 cups fresh or frozen peas

DRESSING:

¼ cup fresh white goat cheese

1 tablespoon fresh lemon juice

½ cup mayonnaise

½ cup plain yogurt or sour cream

1 tablespoon hot-sweet mustard

1½ teaspoons minced fresh thyme, or ½ teaspoon dried thyme

½ cup oil-packed sun-dried tomatoes, drained and cut into strips

8 ounces bacon, cooked until crisp and crumbled

2 cups watercress leaves, coarsely chopped

Salt and freshly ground pepper to taste

COOK MACARONI according to package directions. Drain. Cook fresh peas in salted boiling water for 5 minutes, frozen peas for 3 minutes. Drain under cold water and let cool. **IN A MEDIUM BOWL,** whisk all dressing ingredients together until smooth. In a large bowl, combine remaining ingredients, peas, and macaroni. Toss with dressing. Taste and adjust seasoning. Keep chilled until ready to serve.

ROMANO BEAN, TOMATO, AND MUSHROOM SALAD

With fresh cherry tomatoes both in the salad and whirled into the dressing, this dish is full of summer. Cremini mushrooms, which grow up to be portobellos, have become a real favorite with today's chefs and food editors looking for new and exciting varieties. Ironically, these "Italian brown" mushrooms were about the only ones available until around sixty years ago, when a Pennsylvania grower developed the creamy-white, all-purpose supermarket mushroom and produced it commercially. Fat slices of old-new creminis add their "meat" and earthiness to this salad.

1¹/₂ pounds Romano beans, cut into 2-inch pieces

2 cups cherry tomatoes, halved

12 ounces cremini or white mushrooms, sliced ¹/₄ inch thick

¹/₂ cup chopped fresh parsley

TOMATO-DILL VINAIGRETTE:

4 cherry tomatoes, halved

1 small shallot

1 clove garlic

1 teaspoon grated lemon zest

1 tablespoon fresh lemon juice

1 tablespoon red wine vinegar

¹/₃ cup olive oil

1 tablespoon snipped fresh dill

Salt and freshly ground pepper to taste

COOK BEANS in salted boiling water until crisp-tender, about 3 minutes. Drain under cold water and let cool. **IN A LARGE BOWL,** combine beans, tomatoes, mushrooms, and parsley. In a blender or food processor, process all vinaigrette ingredients until smooth. Toss with bean mixture. Taste and adjust seasoning.

NOTES

DINNER
IN
A BOWL

HEARTY KNIFE-AND-FORK SALADS are homey, big-bowl

attractions that need only some good bread to become a complete meal. Based on beans, legumes, meats, poultry, fish, pasta, or grains, these include inventive interpretations of salads from different culinary traditions and nostalgia-producing treats evocative of Grandma's kitchen.

CURRIED LENTIL
AND ORZO SALAD
WITH ROASTED ROOT VEGETABLES

Lentils are a legume, a plant whose seeds are carried in pods and split in half when ripe. Lentils are also pulses, because they are dried seeds. This relatively low-cost source of protein is often referred to as "poor man's meat." **There are** at least fifty varieties of lentils, ranging in color from rust-brown and loden green to the pretty apricot-colored variety here. These mild-flavored, quickly cooked lentils provide a delicate balance to the roasted root vegetables in this robust vegetable salad, which can be made even heartier with the addition of sliced, cooked sausage.

1 cup red lentils

3 cups water

1 cup orzo pasta

3 tablespoons olive oil

$1/2$ cup chopped fresh parsley

$1/4$ cup chopped fresh cilantro

3 carrots, peeled and diced

2 parsnips, peeled and diced

$1/2$ celery root, peeled and diced

1 large sweet potato, peeled and diced

3 tablespoons minced shallots

1 teaspoon ground cumin

$1/2$ teaspoon salt

DRESSING:

1 teaspoon curry powder or to taste

1 tablespoon chutney

1 tablespoon Dijon mustard

$1/4$ cup rice vinegar

$1/4$ cup olive oil

Salt and freshly ground pepper to taste

IN A MEDIUM SAUCEPAN, bring lentils and water to a boil. Reduce heat to a simmer and cook until lentils are tender, about 15 minutes. Drain and place them in a large bowl. **WHILE THE LENTILS** are cooking, bring a medium saucepan of water to a boil. Add orzo and cook for 10 minutes. Drain and add to lentils. Toss with 1 tablespoon oil and let cool. Stir in parsley and cilantro. **PREHEAT OVEN** to 450°F. In a large bowl, toss carrots, parsnips, celery root, and sweet potato with shallots and remaining 2 tablespoons of oil. Sprinkle with cumin and salt. Spread vegetables in one layer on a sided baking sheet. Roast for about 20 minutes, or until tender and slightly browned. Let cool and add to lentil mixture. Whisk all dressing ingredients together and pour over lentil mixture.

NOTE: If you want an even more substantial salad, add about 8 ounces diced cooked sausage to lentil mixture before tossing with dressing.

THREE-MUSTARD CHICKEN SALAD
WITH RED AND GREEN LETTUCES

serves > 6 to 8

Called the "spice of nations," mustard appears in every culinary tradition. American Indians dried its seeds to use as flavoring and ate the tender raw shoots and lavender flowers of pink mustard. Franciscan padres planted mustard seeds to link the missions they were establishing along the California coast, leaving long, golden "mustard trails" in their wake. **Mustard seeds** come in three popular colors: black, the preferred choice for East Indian dishes, is the most potent and most expensive because it often requires hand harvesting; brown is slightly less pungent and is often substituted for black; and white, or yellow, is often mixed with starch and coloring. Prepared mustard, such as the Dijon and sweet-hot varieties in this recipe, is a mix of seed, salt, vinegar, and often some other liquid, plus additional spices. Together, the three faces of mustard bring heat, sweetness, and texture to this substantial dish.

$2^1/_2$ **pounds skinless, boneless chicken breast halves**

1 cup mayonnaise

3 tablespoons sweet-hot mustard

2 tablespoons Dijon mustard

$^1/_4$ **cup fresh lemon juice**

Salt and freshly ground pepper to taste

4 celery stalks, sliced

$^1/_3$ **cup mustard seeds**

2 tablespoons olive oil

1 head radicchio lettuce, halved and thinly sliced

2 hearts romaine lettuce, 1 thinly sliced

COOK CHICKEN in a covered skillet of salted simmering water for 8 minutes. Remove from heat and let chicken cool completely in covered skillet. Cut chicken into ³/₄-inch cubes and put in a large bowl. In a medium bowl, combine mayonnaise with mustards, lemon juice, salt, and pepper. Combine with chicken and celery. **IN A SMALL SKILLET** over medium high heat, heat olive oil and cook mustard seeds until they stop popping. Add to chicken mixture with radicchio and sliced romaine. Toss gently. Separate leaves from remaining romaine and arrange in a spokelike pattern on a large platter. Mound chicken salad in center.

SINGAPORE NOODLE
AND CRAB SALAD

Any whole East Coast blue crab or West Coast Dungeness makes a good beginning to this salad. You could also use the claws of Florida stone crabs or Alaska king crabs, or the meat of various crabs known as rock, snow, Jonah, red, or the intriguingly named peekytoe. Another option is fresh or frozen crabmeat, usually supplied under the following designations: large, succulent pieces are called lump or jumbo lump; the broken, somewhat smaller, chunks are backfin; and smaller pieces from various parts of the crab are called flaked. They are all delicious in this Singapore-inspired pasta, with its warm and spicy dressing.

DRESSING:

$\frac{1}{2}$ cup chicken stock

$\frac{1}{2}$ cup smooth peanut butter

$\frac{1}{4}$ cup balsamic vinegar

2 tablespoons low-salt soy sauce

1 tablespoon Asian sesame oil

1 tablespoon dry sherry

2 teaspoons sugar

$\frac{1}{2}$ teaspoon Tabasco sauce or to taste

$\frac{1}{4}$ cup chopped scallions

2 tablespoons grated fresh ginger

1 clove garlic, minced

1 pound thin fresh Asian egg noodles

1 bunch scallions, thinly sliced

$\frac{1}{2}$ cup fresh cilantro leaves, coarsely chopped

1 English (hothouse) cucumber, peeled, halved lengthwise, seeded, and thinly sliced

1 red bell pepper, seeded, deribbed, and cut into strips

1 pound cooked fresh crabmeat, picked over for shell and flaked

TO MAKE DRESSING: Bring stock to a boil in a medium saucepan. Remove from heat and add all remaining dressing ingredients. Stir well to blend.

COOK NOODLES in a large pot of salted boiling water for 3 minutes. Drain and let cool. In a large bowl, toss noodles with all remaining ingredients. Add dressing and toss well to combine.

ASPARAGUS, SHRIMP, AND PAPAYA SALAD WITH PAPAYA SEED DRESSING

A native of the American tropics, papaya has been called "the melon that grows on trees." Like melon, this sun-colored fruit/vegetable is delicious in salads, and savvy salad makers also like its tiny charcoal gray seeds for their peppery bite. Here we go one step further, crushing the flavorful seeds into the dressing. When arranged, as suggested, on a large platter, the asparagus, shrimp, and papayas make one of the most beautiful salads in this book.

2 papayas

PAPAYA SEED DRESSING:

$1/3$ cup champagne vinegar

2 teaspoons Dijon mustard

2 tablespoons honey

$1/2$ teaspoon salt

1 tablespoon minced fresh tarragon, or 1 teaspoon
   dried tarragon

$1/4$ cup reserved papaya seeds

$2/3$ cup safflower or vegetable oil

3 pounds asparagus, trimmed and peeled

1 pound medium shrimp, shelled

12 fresh mint leaves for garnish

PEEL AND SEED PAPAYAS, reserving $1/4$ cup of seeds. Dice papaya flesh. In a blender or food processor, combine dressing ingredients and purée until seeds are crushed and mixture is well blended. **IN A LARGE POT** of salted boiling water, cook asparagus for $2^1/2$ minutes, or until crisp-tender. Drain and rinse under cold water until cool to touch. Blot dry with paper towels. Cook shrimp in salted simmering water for 3 minutes. Drain and let cool. **COMBINE ASPARAGUS** with one third of dressing, diced papaya with one third of the dressing, and shrimp with remaining dressing. **ARRANGE ASPARAGUS** on rim of a large serving platter, followed by a circle of diced papaya. Mound shrimp in center. Garnish with mint leaves.

LAMB, WHITE BEAN, AND ARUGULA SALAD WITH CHERRY TOMATO AND ROSEMARY DRESSING

Rosemary, a Mediterranean native whose Latin name means "dew of the sea," is often referred to as the Tuscan herb. It is indispensable in such Italian dishes as the traditional Easter roast lamb, called *abbacchio,* and *pasta e fagioli,* the popular macaroni and bean soup. **With such** credentials, rosemary seems the hands-down choice to unite this salad, which pairs lamb strips and creamy cannellini beans.

2 cups dried cannellini beans, soaked in cold water
   overnight

CHERRY TOMATO AND ROSEMARY DRESSING:
6 cherry tomatoes, halved and seeded
2 cloves garlic
1 1/2 teaspoons fresh minced rosemary, or
   1/2 teaspoon dried rosemary
1/2 teaspoon sugar

3 tablespoons sherry vinegar
1/2 cup olive oil
1/2 teaspoon ground pepper
1/2 teaspoon salt

1 pound cooked lamb, cut into strips
6 cups arugula, torn into bite-sized pieces
Fresh rosemary sprigs for garnish

DRAIN AND COOK BEANS in simmering water until tender, about 45 minutes. Drain and let cool.

IN A BLENDER or food processor, process all dressing ingredients until well blended. In a large bowl, combine lamb, beans, and arugula. Toss with dressing and garnish with sprigs of rosemary.

RED SNAPPER
AND BLACK BEAN SALAD
WITH CHIPOTLE VINAIGRETTE

Chipotle chiles are the tiny but fiery peppers that get their name from the Nahuatl word *poctli,* meaning smoke. They are actually dried jalapeños that are smoked and preserved in vinegar or adobo sauce. Sold in small tins, most are imported from Mexico. Although many other chiles can be used interchangeably, chipotles have a character all their own. As Diana Kennedy says, "There is no substitute." With their natural companions, lime, cilantro, and black beans, they add a distinctive zing to this snapper salad.

1¹/₂ cups dried black beans, soaked in cold water
    overnight

1 cup long-grain rice

VINAIGRETTE:

2 canned chipotle chiles, rinsed and seeded

2 tablespoons fresh lime juice

2 tablespoons white wine vinegar

3 sun-dried tomatoes

¹/₂ teaspoon ground cumin

1 clove garlic

2 tablespoons fresh cilantro leaves

¹/₂ cup corn oil

¹/₂ teaspoon salt

3 pounds snapper fillets

5 fresh tomatillos, husked, cored, and diced

1 red or yellow bell pepper, seeded, deribbed, and
    cut into strips

2 cups watercress or young spinach leaves

DRAIN THE BEANS and cook them in simmering water until tender, about 45 minutes. Drain and let cool. Cook rice in salted simmering water for 18 minutes. Fluff with a fork and let cool. **IN A BLENDER** or food processor, combine all dressing ingredients until well blended. Light a fire in a charcoal grill or preheat a gas grill or broiler. Brush snapper on both sides with some dressing and grill or broil for about 2 minutes on each side, or until opaque throughout. Let cool and cut into strips. **IN A LARGE BOWL,** combine fish, tomatillos, beans, rice, bell pepper, and watercress or spinach leaves and toss with dressing.

NOTE: If fresh tomatillos aren't available, use Roma (plum) tomatoes.

OYSTERS ROCKEFELLER SALAD

serves · 8

A recent visit to New Orleans reminded us that a truly great dish can remain a favorite for a hundred years. Created in 1899 by James Alciatore, owner of Antoine's, the fifty-nine-year-old New Orleans restaurant founded by his father, Oysters Rockefeller has lost none of its vibrancy. **Supposedly** a never-revealed secret, the dish begins with a grand mashing up of puréed spinach, green onions, celery, tarragon, bread crumbs, Tabasco, and butter, splashed with anisette or a reasonable facsimile. A plump spoonful of all this is placed on each oyster, which is put under a broiler and browned. The opulence of the ingredients and taste demanded no less a namesake than John D. Rockefeller—or so they say. This is our saladized version in honor of its centennial.

2 dozen fresh oysters, shucked, liquor reserved

1 tablespoon fresh lemon juice

Vegetable oil for frying

About 1 cup fine fresh bread crumbs

3 tablespoons minced fresh parsley

1 egg, beaten

$1/2$ teaspoon salt

Pinch of cayenne pepper

8 cups spinach leaves, torn into bite-sized pieces

8 ounces bacon, crisply cooked and crumbled

DRESSING:

2 teaspoons Dijon mustard

3 tablespoons fresh lemon juice

2 tablespoons sour cream

1 clove garlic, minced

1 teaspoon minced fresh tarragon

$2/3$ cup olive oil

$1/2$ cup (2 ounces) grated Asiago cheese

IN A MEDIUM SAUCEPAN, bring reserved oyster liquor and lemon juice to a simmer. Add oysters and cook for 2 minutes. Drain and let cool. **IN A LARGE SKILLET,** heat about 2 inches oil over medium-high heat. Combine bread crumbs and parsley. Dip oysters into egg, and then into bread crumbs. Fry until golden brown on all sides, about 4 minutes. Using a slotted spatula, transfer to paper towels to drain. **IN A LARGE BOWL,** combine spinach and bacon. In a medium bowl, whisk all dressing ingredients together. Toss spinach mixture with dressing. Place oysters on top and sprinkle with cheese.

SUMMER COBB SALAD
WITH SWEET CORN AND GREEN BEANS

Many people have heard of Cobb salad but very few are sure what it is. And yet we know exactly when and where it was invented: in 1926 at the Brown Derby Restaurant in Hollywood. And we even know its creator: Robert Cobb, the Derby's owner. The exact ingredients and proportions remain a mystery, however, possibly because Mr. Cobb's real purpose in assembling his first Cobb was mainly to use up leftovers. Perhaps this is why Cobb salad has been called "the ultimate hodgepodge" by such pan-American tasters as Jane and Michael Sterns, who consider it a "study in culinary chaos." Although its contents may vary, the Cobb's most distinguishing characteristic is its form: The ingredients are arranged in rows atop a bed of greens on a flat plate. Here are our two versions, a delicious hodgepodge for each season (see page 166 for Winter Cobb Salad with Roasted Butternut Squash).

1 pound boneless, skinless chicken breasts

2 cups fresh corn kernels (about 4 ears)

1 pound green beans, cut into 1-inch pieces

1 small head iceberg lettuce

1 ripe avocado

2 hard-cooked eggs, chopped

1 pound Roma (plum) tomatoes, seeded and diced (see page 133)

3 scallions, trimmed and thinly sliced

1/2 cup (3 ounces) crumbled ricotta salata cheese

4 ounces bacon, cooked and crumbled

DRESSING:

1 tablespoon fresh lemon juice

1 tablespoon red wine vinegar

1/2 teaspoon anchovy paste

1 teaspoon Dijon mustard

1/2 teaspoon salt

1/2 teaspoon sugar

2/3 cup olive oil

PUT CHICKEN in a medium saucepan and add enough water to cover by 1 inch. Bring to a simmer and cook chicken until opaque throughout, about 8 minutes. Remove from heat and let chicken cool. Cut into $\frac{1}{2}$-inch cubes. **COOK CORN** and beans in salted boiling water for 3 minutes. Drain and let cool. Cut lettuce in half horizontally and cut core from each half. Cut or shred into thin strips. Peel and pit the avocado and cut into $\frac{1}{2}$-inch cubes. Sprinkle with lemon juice. **TO ASSEMBLE** salad, arrange a bed of lettuce on a large platter. Arrange rows of other salad ingredients on top—chicken, avocado, eggs, tomatoes, scallions, corn, green beans, ricotta, and bacon—alternating colors decoratively. **IN A SMALL BOWL,** whisk all dressing ingredients together. Drizzle over salad. Serve immediately.

WINTER COBB SALAD
WITH ROASTED BUTTERNUT SQUASH

$^1/_2$ butternut squash, peeled, seeded, and cut into
$^1/_2$-inch cubes (about 3 cups)

2 golden beets, peeled and cut into $^1/_2$-inch cubes

2 tablespoons olive oil

Salt and freshly ground pepper to taste

1 pound smoked (fully cooked) turkey sausage,
sliced

8 ounces Brussels sprouts, quartered

6 cups spinach leaves, torn into bite-sized pieces

2 heads Belgian endive, cut into thin strips

1 red onion, diced

$^1/_2$ cup (2 ounces) fresh white goat cheese

1 cup (4 ounces) walnut halves, toasted (see
page 32)

DRESSING:

3 tablespoons sherry vinegar

1 tablespoon fresh orange juice

1 tablespoon hot-sweet mustard

$^1/_4$ cup walnut oil

$^1/_4$ cup olive oil

Salt and freshly ground pepper to taste

PREHEAT OVEN to 400°F. In a medium bowl, combine squash, beets, oil, salt, and pepper. Spread mixture on a baking sheet in one layer and roast for 20 minutes. Let cool. **IN A MEDIUM SKILLET,** brown sausage slices over medium-high heat. With a slotted spatula, transfer to paper towels to drain. Cook Brussels sprouts in salted boiling water for 5 minutes. Drain and let cool. **COMBINE** spinach and endives and arrange on a large platter. Arrange rows of other salad ingredients on top: squash, beets, sausage, Brussels sprouts, onion, and goat cheese. Sprinkle with walnuts. Whisk all dressing ingredients together and sprinkle over salad. Serve immediately.

BAJA SALAD
OF SPICY GRILLED SWORDFISH,
AVOCADO, AND CORN

serves > 8

Because of its thick skin and firm, compact flesh, swordfish holds together admirably on the grill. Its meatlike texture takes well to the assertive flavors of hot pepper and cilantro in this marinade, which also serves as a dressing. Tuna and mahi mahi will also work nicely in this recipe, but swordfish makes this a dinner to remember.

MARINADE:

6 tablespoons fresh lime juice

2 tablespoons fresh lemon juice

1 tablespoon white wine vinegar

$1/2$ teaspoon hot pepper sauce

2 scallions, minced

2 tablespoons chopped fresh cilantro

$1/2$ teaspoon salt

$1/2$ cup olive oil

2 pounds swordfish steaks, each about $1/2$-inch thick

2 cups small cherry tomatoes, halved

3 cups fresh corn kernels (about 6 ears)

2 avocados, peeled and pitted

4 cups bite-sized crisp lettuce pieces (romaine, iceberg, frisée, or a mixture)

LIGHT A FIRE in a charcoal grill or preheat a gas grill or broiler. In a medium bowl, combine marinade ingredients. Put swordfish in a shallow nonreactive dish or in a self-sealing plastic bag. Marinate in half of marinade for no more than 30 minutes at room temperature. Grill swordfish for about 3 minutes on each side, or until opaque throughout. Let cool. **CUT SWORDFISH** into cubes and put in a large bowl with tomatoes and corn. Cut 1 avocado into cubes and the other into slices. Add avocado cubes to swordfish mixture. Toss with two thirds of remaining marinade. Combine lettuce with the remaining marinade and spread on platter. Mound swordfish salad over it and garnish with avocado slices.

MANGO-MINT CHICKEN SALAD

According to James Beard, meat salads originated in this country as a catchall for leftovers. Sausages, tongue, ham, and cold corned beef were common, but the real favorite was chicken salad in all its forms. Cooks often used veal and pork as a substitute for chicken, however, which was more expensive and therefore reserved for special occasions. **This chicken salad,** with its Asian and tropical accents, quickly grilled chicken, and crisp-tender vegetables, is a dish tailored to today's taste.

DRESSING:

2 tablespoons fresh lime juice

3 tablespoons fresh lemon juice

1 teaspoon honey

4 fresh mint leaves

1 tablespoon low-salt soy sauce

1 teaspoon grated fresh ginger

6 boneless, skinless chicken breast halves

Salt and freshly ground pepper to taste

6 ounces sugar snap peas, trimmed

4 cups arugula

2 cups pea shoots or bean sprouts

$1/2$ small jicama, peeled and cut into matchsticks

2 small mangos, peeled and cut from pits

Fresh mint sprigs for garnish

IN A BLENDER or food processor, combine all dressing ingredients and purée until well blended. **LIGHT A FIRE** in a charcoal grill or preheat a gas grill or broiler. Pound chicken breasts to flatten slightly and sprinkle with salt and pepper. Brush a little dressing on both sides of chicken and grill or broil for about 4 minutes on each side, or until opaque throughout. Let cool and cut into $\frac{1}{4}$-inch strips. **COOK SNAP PEAS** in boiling salted water for about 30 seconds. Drain and put in ice water to stop cooking and set color. **IN A LARGE BOWL,** combine arugula and sprouts. Moisten with about 2 tablespoons dressing. In another bowl, combine chicken, snap peas, jicama, and mangos. Toss with remaining dressing. Line a platter with arugula mixture. Mound chicken mixture on top. Garnish with mint sprigs.

NOTES

FRUIT
SALADS

SALADS OF FRESH AND DRIED

FRUITS, FRUIT JUICES, AND DRESSINGS MAKE SPARKLING FIRST COURSES, PALATE CLEANSERS BETWEEN COURSES, OR REFRESHING DESSERTS. HERBS, SPICES, AND NUTS ADD INTEREST TO SEASONAL FRUITS, FROM SQUIRTY CITRUS AND FRAGRANT MELONS TO LUSH STONE FRUITS AND PLUMP BERRIES. DEPENDING ON YOUR MENU, YOU'LL FIND SALADS THAT ARE DELICIOUS WITH COOKIES OR CAKE, SOME THAT ARE PERFECT ON A BED OF GREENS, AND A FEW THAT SERVE AS AN ALL-IN-ONE CHEESE AND FRUIT COURSE.

MELON MÉLANGE WITH HONEY-RASPBERRY DRESSING

Melons are like elephants: They're fun and all that, but their sheer size makes them a bit overwhelming. They take days to deal with, especially if, in an excess of summer melon enthusiasm, you buy a couple of varieties in one spree. **Such lack** of control is understandable about this "flower of all fruits," as one poet dubbed the melon, while another praised its pure taste that "charms the throat." In ancient Rome, before they were developed into the many, large, sweet varieties we have today, melons the size of oranges were eaten as salads; they were seasoned with vinegar, pepper, and an unlikely sauce called garum, made from the intestines of anchovies. Melons can also serve as metaphors, as in the adage "Friends are like melons; you have to try fifty of them before you find a good one." In this dessert salad, splashed with the essence of raspberries, they are at their most exquisite.

1 honeydew melon, seeded and flesh removed with a melon ball cutter

1 cantaloupe, seeded and flesh removed with a melon ball cutter

2 cups fresh raspberries

1 cup shelled pistachios

DRESSING:

$^1/_2$ cup fresh raspberries

$^1/_4$ cup fresh lime juice

$^1/_4$ cup honey

1 tablespoon poppy seeds

Toasted pound cake slices or cookies for serving

6 fresh mint sprigs for garnish

IN A LARGE BOWL, combine melons, raspberries, and pistachios. **TO MAKE DRESSING:** Purée raspberries with lime juice and honey. Strain to remove seeds. Stir in poppy seeds. Combine with fruit and garnish with mint. Serve over cake or with cookies.

SUNSHINE CITRUS SALAD
WITH DRIED CHERRIES AND APRICOTS

Breakfast salads haven't yet attained the dubious quality of being "trendy," but salad for brunch is a distinct possibility. In the vague time zone defined by brunch, it is still not too late for a morning infusion of citrus, but something more flamboyant than the traditional glass of o.j. is definitely in order. Enter this salad, a citrus pantheon complete with the exotic blood orange, a less acidic mutation that dates back to seventeenth-century Sicily. Leave out the watercress, and this colorful mélange sparkles as winter dessert.

1 cup dried cherries

$^1/_2$ cup diced dried apricots

1 cup fresh orange juice

2 navel oranges, peeled and sectioned (see
    page 32)

1 blood orange, peeled and sectioned (see page 32)

2 seedless mandarins or tangerines, peeled and
    sectioned (see page 32)

1 grapefruit, peeled and sectioned (see page 32)

1 bunch watercress, stemmed

DRESSING:

$^1/_2$ cup reserved soaking liquid (above)

2 tablespoons sugar

6 fresh mint leaves, chopped

2 tablespoons canola oil

6 fresh mint leaves for garnish

IN A MEDIUM BOWL, soak cherries and apricots in orange juice for 1 hour, or until soft. Drain, reserving $^1/_2$ cup liquid. **IN A LARGE BOWL,** combine cherries, apricots, oranges, mandarins, grapefruit, and watercress. In a small bowl, whisk all dressing ingredients together. Toss with fruit mixture and garnish with mint leaves.

GREEN APPLE, RED GRAPE, AND TOASTED WALNUT SALAD

The Christmas dinner table would be a fitting setting for this sparkling jumble of red and green. This versatile salad makes a festive prelude to a meal, or it can serve as an all-in-one course of cheese, fruit, and nuts. The haunting flavor of walnut oil, which French home cooks once used as freely as olive oil, signifies a special occasion.

3 unpeeled green apples, cored and diced

¼ cup fresh lemon juice

2 cups seedless red grapes, halved

1 cup (4 ounces) walnut pieces, toasted (see
   page 32)

1 cup (5 ounces) crumbled blue cheese

1 tablespoon sweet-hot mustard

¼ cup walnut oil

Leaves from 1 head butter lettuce

IN A MEDIUM BOWL, toss apples with half of lemon juice. Add the grapes, walnuts, and cheese. In a small bowl, whisk remaining lemon juice, mustard, and oil together. Toss with apple mixture. Line plates with lettuce leaves and spoon fruit mixture in center.

STONE FRUIT SALAD WITH CUCUMBER CRESCENTS

Stone fruits are named for their rather convenient anatomy: Their flesh grows around a large pit, or stone. This makes them especially tempting for plain, ordinary eating out-of-hand as well as a good choice for cutting up into salad. In this savory dish, a short marination allows the delicate scent of chervil to make its seductive way into the mix of flavors. Without the taming effects of romaine and cucumbers, this would also make a luscious dessert.

$1^1/_2$ pounds ripe peaches, peeled, pitted, and cut into $^1/_3$-inch wedges

$1^1/_2$ pounds ripe nectarines, pitted and cut into $^1/_3$-inch wedges

1 pound ripe plums, pitted and diced

1 pound ripe apricots, pitted and diced

$^1/_2$ cup fresh lemon juice

$^1/_4$ cup packed light brown sugar

1 tablespoon chopped fresh chervil

1 English (hothouse) cucumber, peeled, halved, and seeded

Leaves from 1 small head romaine lettuce

IN A LARGE BOWL, combine peaches, nectarines, plums, and apricots with lemon juice, brown sugar, and chervil. Refrigerate for 2 hours, stirring occasionally. **CUT CUCUMBER** halves into $^1/_8$-inch slices. Just before serving, toss with fruit mixture. Line each serving plate with 2 lettuce leaves. Fill center of leaves with salad.

MIXED BERRIES WITH
BALSAMIC SPLASH

"Raisins o' the sun"—that was Shakespeare's phrase for currants, which are often used inter-changeably with raisins in the dried state. Named for Corinth, west of Athens, currants come in three main colors: black, used mainly for jams and cassis; the rare white species, a less acidic and conse-quently sweet albino of the red; and tart crimsons, which give this salad its complexity of taste and texture. Without the radicchio, this dish makes a memorable dessert.

4 cups fresh strawberries, hulled and quartered

2 cups fresh raspberries

2 cups fresh blueberries

1 cup fresh red currants, stemmed, (or 1 cup
    additional raspberries)

DRESSING:

3 tablespoons balsamic vinegar

2 tablespoons fresh lime juice

¼ teaspoon ground cinnamon

2 tablespoons honey

2 heads radicchio, quartered, cored, and cut into
    ½-inch shreds

2 teaspoons ground pepper

IN A LARGE BOWL, combine berries and currants. Whisk all dressing ingredients together. In a medium bowl, toss radicchio with 2 tablespoons dressing. Toss remaining dressing with berry mix-ture. Arrange radicchio around edge of a platter. Mound berries in center. Sprinkle with pepper.

MELON, MANGO, AND MINT SALAD WITH PROSCIUTTO STRIPS

serves 8

Salting meat to preserve it has been done for thousands of years. In his cookbook, Apicius, who lived in the first century A.D., provides directions for salt-curing pork, including the encouraging words (here translated from the Latin), "and when ready to use, you'll be surprised." **Not only** surprised but delighted, judging from the continuous popularity of cured hams in many parts of the world, the best of which is arguably the raw, unsmoked ham called *prosciutto crudo,* from the province of Parma. Its lusty yet delicate taste results partly from a diet that includes the whey of Parmesan cheese, as well as from long-curing in the area's mountain air. As an appetite stimulant at the beginning of the meal, thin slices of prosciutto are almost unparalleled, especially in the presence of sweet chunks of melon and mango. In salad form, an underpinning of zippy watercress only makes it better.

1 large Crenshaw or honeydew melon (about 2 pounds), seeded, peeled, and cut into $1/2$-inch chunks

2 ripe mangos, peeled, cut from pit, and cut into $1/2$-inch chunks

$2/3$ cup fresh lemon juice

3 tablespoons sugar

3 tablespoons chopped fresh mint

Pinch of salt

$1/2$ teaspoon ground pepper

$1/4$ cup safflower or vegetable oil

4 cups watercress leaves, coarsely chopped (about 1 bunch)

4 ounces paper-thin prosciutto, cut into strips

$1/2$ cup (2 ounces) pine nuts, toasted (see page 32)

IN LARGE BOWL, combine melon and mango. Stir in 3 tablespoons lemon juice, 2 tablespoons sugar, 2 tablespoons mint, and salt. Let sit for about 10 minutes, tossing occasionally. **IN A SMALL BOWL,** whisk together remaining lemon juice, remaining sugar, remaining mint, pepper, and oil. Place watercress on a platter and drizzle with half of dressing. Stir remaining dressing into melon mixture. Arrange melon mixture over watercress and cover with prosciutto and pine nuts.

PINEAPPLE AND JICAMA SALAD
WITH CRANBERRY DRESSING

Even the most cranberry-weary, holiday-jaded over-eater can usually be revived with this dish. The contrast of juicy, crisp, and chewy is hard to resist in this mix of fresh pineapple, jicama strips, and fresh (or frozen) and dried cranberries. From oakleaf lettuce and cider vinegar to toasted walnuts, this is autumn at its most colorful, in salad form.

$1/2$ cup fresh or frozen cranberries

$1/4$ cup cider vinegar

1 tablespoon honey

1 tablespoon minced shallot

Pinch salt

2 tablespoons walnut oil

1 fresh pineapple, peeled, cored, and cut into
   $1/2$-inch strips

1 large jicama, peeled and cut into matchsticks

$1/2$ cup dried cranberries

1 cup coarsely chopped fresh flat-leaf parsley

Leaves from 1 head red oakleaf lettuce

1 cup coarsely chopped walnuts, toasted (see
   page 32)

IN A SMALL SAUCEPAN, combine fresh or frozen cranberries, vinegar, and honey. Bring to a boil and cook for 1 minute. Reduce heat and simmer until cranberries are soft and juice has thickened, about 5 minutes. In a blender or a food processor, purée mixture and let cool to room temperature. Stir in shallot, salt, and oil. **IN A LARGE BOWL,** toss pineapple with jicama, dried cranberries, and parsley. Toss with cranberry dressing. Line a serving plate with lettuce leaves. Mound fruit on top. Sprinkle with toasted walnuts.

FRESH FIG AND ARUGULA SALAD
WITH GOAT CHEESE TOASTS

With their delicate flesh, smooth as a baby's cheek, and their deep, heady perfume, figs have been enchanting fruit-lovers since the days of Homer in Greece and even earlier in Egypt. Plato himself, not known for flights of culinary abandon, was so passionately involved with the fig that, in the words of Alexis Soyer's *The Pantropheon,* he "ceased to be a philosopher when presented with a basket of that fruit." **To this day** in Provence, bowls of figs are placed on the table as the meal begins so that guests can sample them between each course. This fig-filled salad, topped with a whole fresh fig, usually satisfies the most ardent figophile. Only a combination of both black and green figs might elicit greater joy.

8 fresh green or black figs

6 cups (about 8 ounces) arugula leaves, torn into bite-sized pieces

1 small red onion, diced

8 slices baguette, lightly toasted

¼ cup fresh white goat cheese, at room temperature

DRESSING:

2 tablespoons sherry vinegar

6 tablespoons extra-virgin olive oil

1 teaspoon ground pepper

1 teaspoon honey

PREHEAT BROILER. Quarter 4 figs lengthwise and set aside. Dice remaining figs and combine with arugula and red onion in large bowl. In a small bowl, whisk all dressing ingredients together. Toss with arugula mixture. Spread baguette slices with goat cheese and broil until cheese melts, about 2 minutes. **ARRANGE** arugula mixture on salad plates. Place a quartered fig in center of each salad and 1 goat cheese toast on either side.

GRAPEFRUIT, RED ONION, AND ROMAINE SALAD

In the citrus community, the grapefruit is the new kid on the block. Unlike its thousand-year-old citrus cousins, the grapefruit has been around only a few centuries, probably originating as a mutation somewhere in the West Indies. Called the "forbidden fruit" of Barbados according to Alan Davidson's *Fruit,* the grapefruit is a cross between the orange and the pomelo, from which the French get *pamplemousse,* their word for grapefruit. This also explains the old English word for it—no longer in vogue for obvious reasons—*pimplenose.* The fruit's tendency to grow in clusters, or *grappes,* in French, probably explains the more appetizing English designation, *grapefruit.* **An excellent start** to a meal, this clean-tasting salad reinforces the fruit's reputation as the best way to wake up the taste buds. As you section the grapefruit, work over a bowl to catch the juice and add it to the dressing.

2 grapefruits, peeled and sectioned, juice reserved
   (see page 32)
Leaves from 1 head romaine lettuce
1 red onion, halved and thinly sliced
1 tablespoon white wine vinegar
2 tablespoons sour cream or yogurt
1 tablespoon honey
Pinch of salt

RESERVE 6 outer leaves of romaine and tear rest into bite-sized pieces. In a large bowl, combine grapefruit sections, lettuce, and onion. In a small bowl, combine 2 tablespoons reserved grapefruit juice, vinegar, sour cream, honey, and salt. Whisk to combine and toss with grapefruit mixture. Place a romaine leaf on each salad plate and fill with salad.

FRUIT GAZPACHO SALAD

From the land of gazpacho, an episode from *Don Quixote* shows Sancho Panza becoming impatient with his physicians' remedies and declaring "I would rather stuff myself with gazpachos" than subject himself to any more healthy regimens. Food historian Raymond Sokolov, who has delved deeply into the origins of gazpacho, from its etymology to its ingredients, informs us that the cold soup may have gotten its name from *caspa,* a pre-Roman word for fragment. Before the tomato arrived in Spain, gazpachos contained bits and pieces of ingredients as well as grapes and almonds. Cervantes may have been referring to the tomato-based dish, but he may also have been using gazpachos to mean the crumbs and leftovers upon which the dish was based. **We've taken** our cues from these tantalizing references, adding to our revisionist version more fruits, a lime-based dressing, and the unorthodox New World contribution of Anaheim chiles—a gazpacho for the new millennium. And when making this dish, we follow M. F. K. Fisher's advice on the subject: "I always see to it that I have made too much gazpacho."

1 unpeeled apple, cored and diced

1 unpeeled pear, cored and diced

1 small pineapple, peeled and diced

1 small melon, peeled, cored, and diced

1 cup fresh strawberries, hulled and diced

1 cup seedless red grapes, quartered

1 cup chopped almonds, toasted (see page 32)

1 cucumber, peeled, seeded, and diced

4 scallions, trimmed and thinly sliced

1 Anaheim chile, seeded and diced

3 tablespoons chopped fresh mint

3 tablespoons chopped fresh parsley

3 tablespoons chopped fresh cilantro

1 tablespoon packed brown sugar

2 tablespoons fresh lime juice

IN A LARGE BOWL, combine fruit with almonds, cucumber, onions, chile, mint, parsley, and cilantro. In a small bowl, combine sugar and lime juice. Pour over fruit mixture and mix well to combine.

NOTES

SLENDER
SALADS

TASTY AND LIGHT

CALORIE-CONSCIOUS CONCOCTIONS, THESE SALADS ARE LOW IN CHOLESTEROL AND FAT BUT RICH IN FLAVOR. THEY MAKE PERFECT LUNCHES AND NUTRITIOUS, DIET-FRIENDLY SUPPERS AND SNACKS.

DRESSINGS

EVEN the leanest assemblage of salad ingredients can be subverted by a dribble of innocent-looking dressing: All it takes is an excess of oil used to balance out the vinegar or other acid component. Ironically, the best solution is to modify the amount or type of acid, because this will allow the addition of less oil. In our slender salads, we make judicious use of citrus juices, balsamic or sherry vinegar, and fruit-infused wine-vinegars that are either lower in acid or highly flavorful. These dressings get a splurge of flavor from fresh herbs and puréed fruits and vegetables, which provide lots of body but no fat. We're also fond of adding a bit of soft cheese like goat or Neufchâtel, and/or some yogurt or buttermilk, to produce a rich creaminess. Because buttermilk and yogurt are interchangeable in these recipes, personal preference or availability can dictate your choice. A splash of stock or water extends the dressing nicely with no additional oil.

PRECEDING each dressing are suggestions for the greens, vegetables, or fruits that best complement the ingredients. We also include our three "Umpteen" salads, so called because, among family and friends, they are the hands-down favorites—despite the fact that we've served them umpteen times.

BASIC LOW-FAT VINAIGRETTE

Because balsamic vinegar has an intrinsic sweetness and is much less acidic than other vinegars; it isn't overwhelmed by oil. Paired with an equal amount of oil, it produces a fully flavored balsamic taste, while a tablespoon of stock or water enhances the volume. Try this dressing with red-tinged greens tossed with a flurry of Belgian endive leaves.

2 tablespoons balsamic vinegar

2 tablespoons olive oil

1 tablespoon water or stock

1 small clove garlic

Salt and freshly ground pepper to taste

IN A FOOD PROCESSOR or blender, process all ingredients until emulsified. Taste and adjust seasoning. Store in an airtight container in the refrigerator for up to 1 week.

ORANGE-MUSTARD VINAIGRETTE

makes about 1/2 cup

This is excellent with a mix of pungent greens and fruit, such a winter salad of spinach and orange sections. Choose a different mustard each time—grainy, hot-sweet, Dijon, herb-infused—to change the flavor.

$1/4$ cup fresh orange juice

1 tablespoon fresh lemon juice

2 tablespoons minced shallots

1 tablespoon grainy mustard

2 tablespoons olive oil

$1/2$ teaspoon honey

Salt and freshly ground pepper to taste

IN BLENDER or food processor, process all ingredients until emulsified. Taste and adjust seasoning. Store in an airtight container in the refrigerator for up to 1 week.

BALSAMIC AND ROASTED GARLIC VINAIGRETTE

Roasted garlic gives both a sweet, nutty flavor and a creamy texture here. Try this on soft-leaf lettuces and, for a more substantial meal, add sliced chicken breast.

3 cloves roasted garlic, squeezed from their skins
   (see note)
2 tablespoons balsamic vinegar
2 tablespoons vegetable or chicken stock
2 tablespoons olive oil
$1/2$ teaspoon minced fresh rosemary, or $1/4$ teaspoon
   dried rosemary
Salt and freshly ground pepper to taste

IN A FOOD PROCESSOR or blender, process all ingredients until emulsified. Taste for salt and pepper. Store in an airtight container in the refrigerator for up to 5 days.

ROASTING GARLIC: Preheat oven to 400° F. Cut top third from bulb of garlic. Wrap in foil and roast about 40 minutes, or until garlic is soft.

SUN-DRIED TOMATO VINAIGRETTE

makes about ¾ cup

The combination of sun-dried and fresh tomatoes makes this a great choice for pasta salads—any shape—warm or at room temperature.

4 dry-packed sun-dried tomatoes, soaked in hot
   water 20 minutes or until soft
1 tomato, seeded and chopped (see page 133)
6 fresh basil leaves
1 clove garlic
1 tablespoon olive oil
Salt and freshly ground pepper to taste

REMOVE 2 tablespoons of tomato soaking water and reserve. In a food processor or blender, purée both tomatoes, basil, garlic, reserved soaking water, and olive oil until emulsified. Taste and adjust seasoning. Store in an airtight container in the refrigerator up to 1 week.

CREAMY YOGURT DRESSING

This dressing is wonderful on steamed vegetables, such as asparagus or broccoli, and also as a dip for cut-up raw vegetables.

1/2 cup nonfat plain yogurt

2 tablespoons mayonnaise

1 tablespoon fresh lemon juice

1 tablespoon sweet-hot mustard

1 tablespoon snipped fresh dill

1 teaspoon minced fresh tarragon

Salt and freshly ground pepper to taste

IN A SMALL BOWL, whisk all ingredients together until well blended. Taste and adjust seasoning. Refrigerate in an airtight container for up to 3 days.

HONEY "CREAM" DRESSING

makes about ⅓/ cup

In this dressing, which is spectacular on fruit salads or as a dip for fresh strawberries, cottage cheese imparts a lush undertone. For more richness and a denser texture, you can substitute ricotta.

$1/2$ cup low-fat or nonfat cottage cheese

1 tablespoon honey

1 tablespoon fresh lime juice

2 tablespoons poppy seeds

IN A BLENDER, purée cottage cheese until smooth. Transfer to a small bowl and whisk in honey, lime juice, and poppy seeds. Refrigerate in an airtight container for up to 3 days.

HERB-BUTTERMILK DRESSING

We call this our picnic dressing: great on potato salad, coleslaw, or a toss of al dente vegetables.

1 cup watercress leaves

2 tablespoons snipped fresh dill

¼ cup fresh parsley sprigs

1 bunch chives

4 fresh mint leaves

1 cup buttermilk

1 tablespoon prepared horseradish

Pinch of sugar

Salt and freshly ground pepper to taste

IN A BLENDER or food processor, purée watercress, dill, parsley, chives, and mint. Add buttermilk, horseradish, and sugar and process just until blended. Add salt and pepper. Refrigerate in an airtight container for up to 3 days.

FRESH GINGER AND SESAME DRESSING

Tang and nuttiness make this a perfect choice for Asian pasta salads, rice salads, or a mixture of steamed vegetables.

1 clove garlic, minced

3 scallions, white parts only, finely chopped

1-inch piece fresh ginger, peeled and grated

2 tablespoons rice wine vinegar

1 tablespoon low salt soy sauce

1 tablespoon Asian sesame oil

1 teaspoon packed brown sugar

IN A SMALL BOWL, whisk all ingredients together until well blended. Refrigerate in an airtight container for up to 5 days.

CITRUS-CHILE DRESSING

This cumin-scented mixture brightens up just about anything, from a humble black bean and corn salad to an imposing grilled fish served with the freshest seasonal greens.

1 jalapeño chile, seeded

2 tablespoons fresh cilantro leaves

2 tablespoons fresh orange juice

2 tablespoons fresh lemon juice

1 tablespoon fresh lime juice

½ teaspoon ground cumin

2 tablespoon olive oil

Salt to taste

IN A BLENDER or food processor, purée all ingredients until smooth. Taste and adjust seasoning. Refrigerate in an airtight container for up to 5 days.

GOAT CHEESE DRESSING

The sultry magic of goat cheese makes spears of romaine or any mix of seasonal greens downright irresistible.

2 tablespoons fresh white goat cheese

1 1/2 teaspoons minced fresh thyme, or 1/2 teaspoon
   dried thyme

1/2 teaspoon dried oregano

1/4 cup fresh lemon juice

2 tablespoons water

Salt and freshly ground pepper to taste

IN A BLENDER or food processor, purée all ingredients until smooth. Taste and adjust seasoning. Refrigerate in an airtight container for up to 2 days.

GRAPEFRUIT AND SHRIMP SALAD
WITH HONEY-SOY DRESSING

Maybe it's the delicately pink grapefruit sections, but this salad always seems perfect for a spring luncheon or as a prelude to a light meal. You may have to look in the Asian ingredients section of the supermarket for hot chile oil—how hot depends on the brand.

1 pound medium shrimp, shelled

DRESSING:

1 tablespoon Asian sesame oil

1 tablespoon honey

2 tablespoons balsamic vinegar

1 tablespoon low-salt soy sauce

$1/8$ teaspoon hot chile oil

3 tablespoons vegetable stock or water

4 cups fresh spinach, leaves torn into bite-sized pieces

2 small pink grapefruits, peeled and sectioned (see page 32)

4 scallions, thinly sliced

COOK SHRIMP in salted simmering water for 3 minutes. Drain and let cool. In a small bowl, whisk all dressing ingredients together until well blended. **ON A SERVING PLATTER,** make a bed of spinach leaves. Sprinkle with a few tablespoons of dressing. Arrange grapefruit sections and shrimp over spinach and drizzle with remaining dressing. Sprinkle with scallions.

SHREDDED CABBAGE AND CRAB SALAD
WITH ORANGE-MUSTARD DRESSING

This updated coleslaw has a mouth-tingling spiciness and crunch that make it particularly refreshing. Things only get better with the topping of sweet crabmeat mixed with capers.

DRESSING:

³/₄ cup plain low-fat yogurt

¹/₄ cup fresh orange juice

3 tablespoons hot-sweet mustard

¹/₂ teaspoon Asian sesame oil

1 napa cabbage, cored and shredded

4 carrots, peeled and shredded

1 small radicchio, shredded

1 fennel bulb, trimmed, cored, and very thinly
   sliced

¹/₄ cup snipped fresh dill

1 pound fresh lump crabmeat, picked over for shell

¹/₄ cup capers, drained and rinsed

Salt and freshly ground pepper to taste

¹/₄ cup toasted sesame seeds (see page 32)

IN A SMALL BOWL, whisk all dressing ingredients together. In a large bowl, combine cabbage, carrots, radicchio, fennel, and half of the dill. Toss with ³/₄ cup of the dressing. **IN A SMALL BOWL,** combine crabmeat, capers, remaining dill, and remaining dressing. Add salt and pepper. Arrange cabbage on a platter or individual plates. Top with crab mixture and sprinkle with sesame seeds.

SPRING GREENS AND
STRAWBERRY SALAD

A few minutes of marinating in a balsamic dressing augments the luscious strawberriness of this salad, which has definite romantic sensibilities.

DRESSING:

4 large strawberries, hulled

2 tablespoons balsamic vinegar

1 tablespoon fresh orange or lemon juice

1 teaspoon sugar

1 tablespoon vegetable oil

4 fresh mint leaves, chopped

2 cups fresh strawberries

4 cups mixed salad greens

$1/_3$ cup (2 ounces) crumbled fresh white goat cheese

IN A BLENDER or food processor, purée all dressing ingredients. Reserve 4 of strawberries for garnish; hull and slice the rest. Toss sliced strawberries with dressing and let sit for about 15 minutes. Combine strawberry mixture and greens. Place salad on plates and sprinkle with goat cheese. Garnish each plate with 1 reserved berry.

MELON, JICAMA, AND SHRIMP SALAD

serves > 8

A few years ago, cookbook author Laurel Robertson described jicama as a "stranger . . . in the produce section." But now, this homely-looking blob of a vegetable has become familiar as an ingredient in salads, crudités, and salsas. A member of the morning-glory family, jicama is a cousin to the sweet potato and a native of Mexico and South America. Like hot pretzels on the sidewalks of New York, jicama is a street food in its homeland, served with a squeeze of lime and a shake of fiery chile powder. Low in starch and calories, it is a good foundation for a slender salad.

DRESSING:

1/4 cup fresh orange juice

2 tablespoons fresh lime juice

1 jalapeño chile, seeded and minced

3 tablespoons olive oil

4 small ripe cantaloupes (or other small sweet
   melons)

1 large jicama, peeled and cut into sticks

1 pound bay shrimp

6 fresh mint leaves, coarsely chopped

1/4 cup chopped fresh cilantro

1/4 cup chopped fresh parsley

Salt and freshly ground pepper to taste

8 fresh mint sprigs for garnish

IN A SMALL BOWL, whisk all dressing ingredients together until well blended. Cut melons in half and scoop out flesh with a melon baller, reserving shells. In a large bowl, combine melon with jicama, shrimp, mint leaves, cilantro, and parsley. Toss with dressing and add salt and pepper. Serve in melon shells, garnished with mint.

STONE FRUIT AND GREENS WITH GOAT CHEESE DRESSING

Rich and sweet and juicy and garden-fresh, the ingredients for this salad are luscious even in their undressed state. Give them a toss with the just-tart-enough taste of goat cheese and you'll be facing a whole new dilemma: Should you serve this as a pre-meal fruit cup or after the main course, possibly with a plate of cheese on the side? Or perhaps as a light lunch or an impromptu backyard picnic on a sunny day? With this dish, as long as it's summer, you can't go wrong.

DRESSING:

¼ cup fresh white goat cheese

3 tablespoons plain yogurt

1 tablespoon olive oil

1 tablespoon fresh lemon juice

1 teaspoon minced fresh thyme, or ½ teaspoon
  dried thyme

2 plums

2 apricots

1 peach

1 nectarine

8 cups mixed salad greens

1 cup (5 ounces) pine nuts, toasted (see page 32)

IN A SMALL BOWL, whisk all dressing ingredients together. Pit fruit and cut into 1-inch chunks, reserving juices. **IN A LARGE BOWL,** combine fruit with greens and half of pine nuts. Stir 2 to 3 tablespoons reserved fruit juices into dressing. Pour over salad and toss. Sprinkle with remaining pine nuts.

ASPARAGUS, RADISH, AND MUSHROOM SALAD

Just tossing this salad, with its morning-fresh fragrance and color, rewards you with the pleasure of spring. A kaleidoscope of flavors, from delicate to assertive, peppery to sweet, adds to this light but satisfying dish.

1 pound thin asparagus, trimmed, peeled, and very thinly sliced on the diagonal

8 red radishes, halved lengthwise and thinly sliced

8 ounces mushrooms, stemmed and thinly sliced

2 bunches watercress, stemmed and coarsely chopped

1 bunch chives, cut into ¼-inch pieces

½ cup (3 ounces) Asiago cheese, shaved with a vegetable peeler

DRESSING:

2 tablespoons fresh lemon juice

1 tablespoons fresh orange juice

1 tablespoon balsamic vinegar

3 tablespoons olive oil

1 teaspoon sweet hot mustard

Salt and freshly ground pepper

IN A LARGE BOWL, combine asparagus, radishes, mushrooms, watercress, chives, and cheese. In a small bowl, whisk dressing ingredients together until well blended. Toss with salad. Taste and adjust for seasoning.

SWEET AND SLENDER SALAD

Like so many dishes that are more than the sum of their parts, this one begins with a ramble around a farmer's market, or a stop at a country roadside stand on a sun-filled Saturday. There, from the weathered wood table, gather your ingredients: ears of corn, warm from the fields; some sassy chervil; a jewel box of Sweet 100s bursting with sugar. Don't forget a nice fat clump of pea shoots, also known as pea sprouts, pea greens, or pea vine shoots. A few minutes in the kitchen and you'll have a beauty of a salad, a summer day served up on a red lettuce leaf.

2 cups fresh sweet peas

2 cups fresh sweet corn kernels (about 4 ears)

2 cups Sweet 100 cherry tomatoes, halved

2 cups pea shoots or bean sprouts

¼ cup chopped fresh chervil or parsley

1 tablespoon celery seed

2 tablespoons balsamic vinegar

Salt and freshly ground pepper to taste

8 red leaf lettuce cups

DRESSING:

3 tablespoons low-fat or non-fat plain yogurt

2 tablespoons mayonnaise

COOK PEAS in salted boiling water for 4 minutes; rinse under cold water. Cook corn in salted boiling water for 3 minutes; rinse under cold water. In a large bowl, combine tomatoes, peas, corn, sprouts, and chervil. In a small bowl, whisk all dressing ingredients. Toss with tomato mixture. Taste and adjust seasoning. Mound in lettuce cups.

RED-HOT SALAD

Red can signify fire or smoke or heat, but in this salad it's all of the above. Sparkling with color, the strips and slices of bright red vegetables make a racy spectacle, even as a still life. Warming spices in a lemon-tinged dressing do nothing to detract from the excitement.

2 pounds large red bell peppers, roasted, peeled, and cut into strips (see page 32)

2 pounds tomatoes, halved, seeded, and cut into thin wedges

1 red jalapeño chile, seeded and cut into very fine strips

DRESSING:

2 cloves garlic, minced

$^1/_2$ teaspoon ground cumin

$^1/_2$ teaspoon ground coriander

$^1/_2$ teaspoon paprika

$1^1/_2$ teaspoons minced fresh thyme, or $^1/_2$ teaspoon dried thyme

2 tablespoons olive oil

1 tablespoon balsamic vinegar

1 tablespoon fresh lemon juice

Salt and freshly ground pepper to taste

IN A LARGE BOWL, combine bell peppers, tomatoes, and jalapeño. In a small bowl, whisk all dressing ingredients together. Toss with vegetables. Taste and adjust seasoning.

WARM MUSHROOM SALAD

There's nothing like the tempting chunkiness of cut-up mushrooms to make you forget their lean and virtuous nature. A quick sauté releases their unctuous flavors and accents their rich, velvety texture. Served warm in its mustardy dressing, this mushroom mixture easily becomes a satisfying, light meal.

DRESSING:

1 tablespoon walnut oil

1 tablespoon olive oil

1 tablespoon balsamic vinegar

1 tablespoon olive oil

1 tablespoon yellow mustard seed

1 tablespoon brown mustard seed

1 shallot, sliced

1 pound mixed mushrooms (such as cremini, portobellos, and stemmed shiitakes), sliced

3 cups torn butter lettuce leaves

3 cups torn mustard green leaves

Salt and freshly ground pepper to taste

IN A SMALL BOWL, whisk all dressing ingredients together. In a non-stick skillet, heat oil over medium heat and cook mustard seeds until they begin to pop. Add shallot and cook for about 2 minutes. Add mushrooms and cook over high heat for about 5 minutes. **IN A LARGE BOWL,** combine mushrooms and greens and toss with dressing. Add salt and pepper. Serve warm.

NOTES

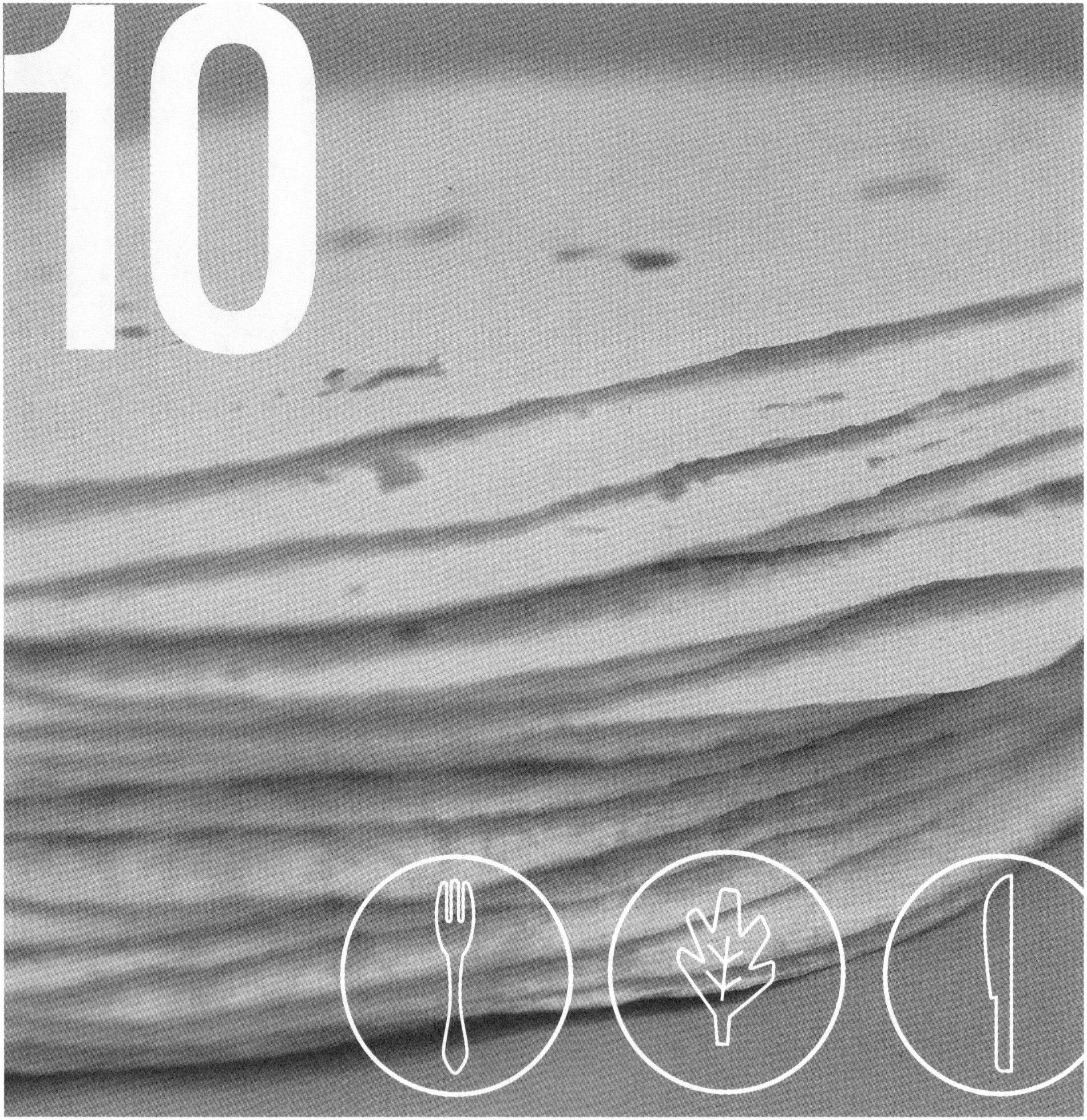
10

WRAPPED

INSPIRATION FOR WRAPPED salads comes from some of the world's oldest cuisines and most venerable traditions. These include Indonesian lumpia, Vietnamese rice paper rolls, Chinese popiah, and all kinds of wontons, pot stickers, and spring rolls. Other models include Russian piroshki, Indian samosas, French pan bagnat, Italian calzone, Cornish pasties, the Hungarian cheese buns called *turos delkli,* Middle Eastern pita and Aram sandwiches, and all the Greek delicacies wrapped in phyllo. Even pancakes in all their ethnicities work as wrappers, whether they're Italian crespelle, French crêpes, Russian blini, Swedish *plattar,* or Korean *koo chuyl pan.* Closer to home, we have empanadas from all over Latin America, while Mexico alone contributes burritos, chalupas, tortillas, and chimichangas. Because wraps are so effective as palate-awakening packages of tantalizing tastes, textures, and aromas, they make excellent salads. WHATEVER their final form, all wraps are simply flour mixed with some form of liquid: water, milk, oil, butter, eggs. In this chapter, any filling will work equally well in any wrapping device, unless otherwise indicated.

SALADS

SHRIMP AND FETA CHEESE SALAD

makes 6 pita pockets

Crumbled feta cheese brings tang and texture to this colorful tumble of shrimp, tomatoes, and fresh chopped zucchini.

8 ounces cooked shrimp, chopped

2 small firm zucchini, coarsely chopped

2 Roma (plum) tomatoes, coarsely chopped

$^3/_4$ cup (4 ounces) crumbled feta cheese

2 tablespoons fresh lemon juice

3 tablespoons olive oil

1 teaspoon dried oregano

1 cup chopped fresh parsley

Salt and freshly ground pepper to taste

6 mini pita breads

IN A MEDIUM BOWL, combine all ingredients except pita. Taste and adjust seasoning. Make a slit in one side of each pita bread and fill.

RATATOUILLE AND SPINACH

Don't let the simplicity of this stove-top ratatouille fool you: The mixture is full of the flavor and character of the classic version, and the spinach leaves add a subtle, fresh taste.

2 tablespoons olive oil

1 onion, diced

1 clove garlic, minced

1 small eggplant, diced

1 small red bell pepper, seeded, deribbed and
   diced

4 ounces small cremini mushrooms, quartered

1 cup chopped tomatoes

$1/2$ teaspoon dried thyme

$1/4$ cup chopped fresh basil

Salt and freshly ground pepper to taste

Six 6-inch pita breads, cut in half to make
   12 pockets

3 cups spinach leaves, coarsely chopped

IN A MEDIUM SKILLET over medium-high heat, heat oil and sauté onion, garlic, eggplant, pepper, and mushrooms until slightly softened, about 5 minutes. Stir in tomatoes and thyme, cover, and simmer for 8 minutes. Uncover and simmer another 5 minutes. Stir in basil. Let cool and add salt and pepper. Line pita halves with spinach and fill with ratatouille.

FARMER'S SALAD

The creamy appearance of this filling gives little indication of the peppery crunch of radish and cucumber that lies in wait.

2 cups red radishes, diced

1 English (hothouse) cucumber, peeled, seeded,
   and diced

6 scallions, thinly sliced

1 cup lowfat cottage cheese

3 tablespoons plain yogurt

1/2 teaspoon paprika

2 tablespoons snipped fresh dill

Salt and freshly ground pepper to taste

Six 6-inch pita breads, cut in half to make 12
   pockets

Oakleaf lettuce leaves

IN A MEDIUM BOWL, combine radishes, cucumber, and scallions. In a small bowl, combine cottage cheese, yogurt, paprika, and dill. Add to vegetables and mix well. Add salt and pepper. Line pita halves with lettuce leaves and fill with salad.

EXTRAVAGANT EGG SALAD

People who find plain old egg salad irresistible can hardly believe their good fortune when they taste this new, improved, luxury model, enlivened with smoked salmon, capers, and sun-dried tomatoes.

8 hard-cooked eggs

6 oil-packed sun-dried tomatoes, drained and cut
    into strips

2 tablespoons capers, drained and rinsed

3 ounces smoked salmon, cut into thin strips

2 tablespoons minced shallot

$\frac{1}{2}$ cup mayonnaise

1 tablespoon sherry vinegar

Salt and freshly ground pepper to taste

Six 6-inch pita breads, cut in half to make
    12 pockets

2 cups mixed salad greens

IN A LARGE BOWL, mash eggs. Combine with tomatoes, capers, salmon, and shallots. In a small bowl, mix mayonnaise with vinegar. Add to egg mixture and mix well to combine. Add salt and pepper. Line pita pockets with greens and fill with egg salad.

BLACK BEAN, RED PEPPER, AND CHICKEN SALAD

Roasted peppers, sultry black beans, and fresh cilantro lend an unmistakably Mexican piquancy to this salad, which is enticing wrapped or unwrapped.

2 cups dried black beans, soaked in cold water
   overnight

DRESSING:

2 tablespoons fresh lime juice

3 tablespoons red wine vinegar

1 teaspoon ground cumin

$1/8$ teaspoon cayenne pepper

$1/2$ cup corn or canola oil

2 red bell peppers, roasted, peeled, and cut into
   strips (see page 32)

2 cups diced cooked chicken

2 cups diced Roma (plum) tomatoes

$1/2$ cup coarsely chopped fresh cilantro

1 small red onion, chopped

Salt and freshly ground pepper to taste

Six 10-inch flour tortillas

2 cups (8 ounces) shredded Cheddar or jack cheese

1 head iceberg lettuce, cored and shredded

DRAIN BEANS. Cook in salted simmering water until tender, about 45 minutes. Drain and let cool. **IN A SMALL BOWL,** whisk all dressing ingredients together. In a large bowl, combine beans, peppers, chicken, tomatoes, cilantro, and onion. Toss with dressing and add salt and pepper. **TOP EACH** flour tortilla with some cheese and then lettuce. Spread some chicken filling over lettuce. Tuck in sides and roll like a cigar. Cut in half on the diagonal.

GRILLED CHICKEN CAESAR WRAP

Plump strips of chicken straight from the grill transform this Caesar into a meal. For a last-minute lunch, you could substitute sliced turkey or chicken straight from the deli.

8 skinless, boneless chicken breast halves

Salt and freshly ground pepper to taste

2 tablespoons olive oil

$^1/_4$ cup mayonnaise

$^1/_4$ cup (2 ounces) grated Parmesan cheese

3 anchovy fillets, minced

1 clove garlic, minced

1 teaspoon Dijon mustard

1 tablespoon fresh lemon juice

Eight 10-inch flour tortillas

1 large head romaine, cut into shreds

LIGHT A FIRE in a charcoal grill or preheat a gas grill or broiler. Sprinkle chicken breasts with salt and pepper and brush both sides with oil. Grill about 4 minutes per side. Cool and cut into strips. **IN A MEDIUM BOWL,** whisk mayonnaise, cheese, anchovies, garlic, mustard, and lemon juice together. **SPREAD** tortillas with this mixture. Arrange chicken and romaine over the dressing. Tuck in sides and roll up like a cigar. Cut in half diagonally.

GORGONZOLA AND GREENS WRAP

Nothing mysterious about the appeal here: The crisp sweetness of fruit plays off the salty richness of cheese and ham.

4 ounces (1 cup) Gorgonzola cheese at room
    temperature
2 tablespoons extra-virgin olive oil
4 ounces mixed salad greens, torn into bite-sized
    pieces
4 ounces prosciutto, cut into strips
2 unpeeled apples, cored and diced
Four 10-inch flour tortillas

IN A SMALL BOWL, blend cheese with olive oil until smooth. In a large bowl, combine greens, prosciutto, and apples. Spread tortillas with cheese mixture and then with greens mixture. Tuck sides in and roll up like a cigar. Cut in half on the diagonal.

PAN BAGNAT

SERVES 4

Maybe it's stretching the definition to call pan bagnat a wrap, but one bite of this exalted tuna sandwich will put you in a forgiving mood. The name of this Provençal favorite, "bathed bread," refers to bread that is "bathed" in the olive oil in the filling.

1 long baguette

1 tablespoon olive oil

2 cups chopped tomatoes, drained

1 clove garlic, minced

1 cup niçoise olives, pitted and coarsely chopped

2 tablespoons capers, drained and rinsed

1 small red onion, diced

Two 7-ounce cans oil-packed tuna, drained and
   flaked

1 bunch watercress, stemmed and coarsely chopped

3 tablespoons chopped fresh parsley

3 tablespoons red wine vinegar

$\frac{1}{4}$ cup extra-virgin olive oil

Salt and freshly ground pepper to taste

CUT OFF top third of the baguette lengthwise. Hollow out centers, saving about 2 cups of crumbs. Brush inside of baguette lightly with oil. In a large bowl, combine crumbs with all remaining ingredients. Add salt and pepper. **FILL BAGUETTE** bottom with crumb mixture. Cover with top and press down. Cut into 4 equal sections and wrap each in plastic wrap. Refrigerate for 2 to 3 hours before serving. Let stand at room temperature 1 hour before serving.

NOTES

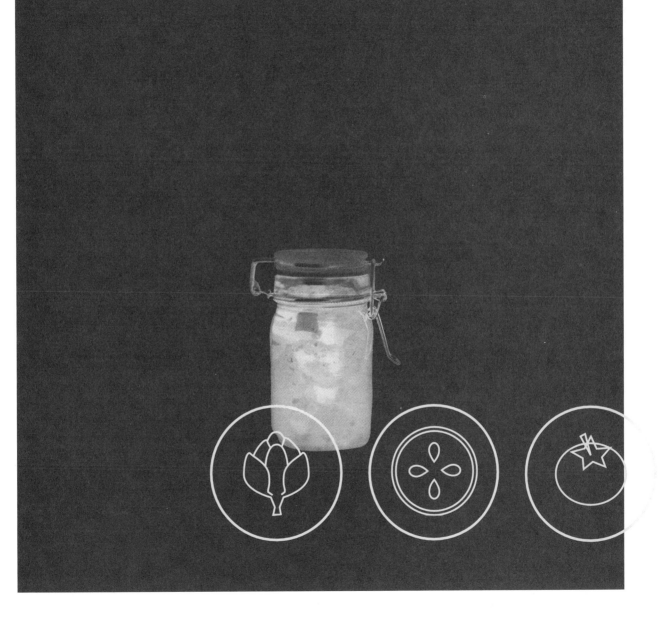

THESE SALADS CAN BE

made on a moment's notice from foods kept on hand in your pantry, refrigerator, and freezer. Some of the most useful items to keep in stock include a variety of mustards, vinegars, and olive oils; several types of rice (Arborio, basmati, brown, wild); dried fruits; shaped pastas, noodles, couscous; canned beans, bottled artichokes, jars of roasted peppers, oil-packed tuna; frozen peas. In addition to their place in the following recipes, these ingredients can be valuable in creating an exciting meal or transforming an ordinary dish, especially at the last minute.

GARBANZO AND
MARINATED-ARTICHOKE SALAD

Tossed with al dente, tube-shaped pasta, this mix of bean, olive, and artichoke is a deliciously edible study in texture. Permeated with artichoke flavor from the marinade, the spicy-sweet dressing brings a lively freshness to this readily made salad.

8 ounces penne pasta

2 jars marinated artichokes, drained, and marinade reserved

One 16-ounce can garbanzo beans, drained and rinsed

1 cup imported black olives, pitted and halved

¹/₂ cup chopped fresh parsley

DRESSING:

3 tablespoons reserved artichoke marinade (above)

1 teaspoon sweet-hot mustard

1 tablespoon fresh lemon juice

2 tablespoons olive oil

Salt and freshly ground pepper to taste

COOK pasta according to package directions. Drain and let cool. Cut artichoke hearts into quarters. In a large bowl, combine artichokes, penne, beans, olives, and parsley. In a small bowl, whisk all dressing ingredients together until well combined. Toss with artichoke mixture. Taste and adjust seasoning.

"PEARLS" AND PEAS

The Israeli couscous in this salad is tiny pearls of pasta toasted an appetizing light brown. Once found exclusively on restaurant menus, this versatile ingredient began to appear in supermarkets in the kosher food section. It has since been traveling the aisles and can now also be found in the pasta section and/or with the "gourmet" foods. Wherever you find it, you'll enjoy the delighted looks on your guests' faces when you serve this unusual vegetable and pasta salad.

1 pound Israeli couscous (pearl pasta)

One 10-ounce package frozen peas, cooked according to package directions, drained, and cooled

6 scallions, trimmed and sliced

1 zucchini, diced

1/2 cup watercress leaves, coarsely chopped

DRESSING:

1/2 cup pesto, homemade (recipe follows) or store bought

2 tablespoons mayonnaise

1 tablespoon fresh lemon juice

Salt and freshly ground pepper to taste

10 fresh basil leaves for garnish

COOK couscous according to package directions. Drain and let cool. In a large bowl, combine pasta, peas, scallions, zucchini, and watercress. In a small bowl, whisk all dressing ingredients together until well blended. Combine with pasta mixture. Taste for salt and pepper. Garnish with basil leaves.

PESTO: In a blender or food processor, combine 1 cup fresh basil leaves, 3 cloves garlic, 1/2 cup toasted pine nuts, 1/3 cup grated Parmesan cheese, and 1/3 cup olive oil. Process until a rough paste is formed. Taste for salt and pepper.

ORIENT EXPRESS SALAD

A bowl of these noodles glinting with crescents of cucumber looks like a mild-mannered dish at first glance. Move closer, however, and the toasty aroma of sesame oil and the assertive tang of fresh ginger begin to reveal the true racy nature of this Asian-inspired salad.

One 12-ounce package fresh thin Chinese egg
    noodles (found in refrigerated section of grocery
    stores)
6 scallions, thinly sliced
1 English (hothouse) cucumber, peeled, halved
    lengthwise, seeded, and sliced
$1/2$ cup fresh cilantro leaves, coarsely chopped
$1/2$ cup dry-roasted peanuts, coarsely chopped

DRESSING:

2 tablespoons rice vinegar
1 tablespoon Asian sesame oil
1 tablespoon low-salt soy sauce
1 tablespoon grated fresh ginger
1 clove garlic, minced
2 tablespoons fresh lemon juice
$1/2$ teaspoon hot pepper sauce

IN A LARGE POT of salted boiling water, cook noodles for 2 minutes. Drain in a colander and rinse under cold running water until cool to the touch. Drain again. In a large bowl, combine noodles with scallions, cucumber, cilantro, and half of peanuts. **IN A SMALL BOWL,** whisk all dressing ingredients together until well combined. Toss with noodles. Sprinkle with remaining peanuts and serve.

WHITE BEAN, TUNA, AND TOMATO SALAD

The fragile perfume of tarragon wends its way through the creaminess and crunch of this tempting combination. Though any tuna works well here, an imported olive-oil-packed brand makes this off-the-shelf combination almost elegant. Even if it is drained and rinsed to remove excess oil, tuna packed in oil—any oil—has infinitely more taste than water-packed.

Two 16-ounce cans cannellini (white beans),
    drained and rinsed

Two 7-ounce cans tuna, drained and flaked

2 celery stalks, thinly sliced

$1/2$ cup oil-packed sun-dried tomatoes, drained and
    cut into strips

$1/2$ cup chopped fresh parsley

DRESSING:

2 tablespoons tarragon mustard

2 tablespoons fresh lemon juice

2 tablespoons balsamic vinegar

$1/2$ cup olive oil

Salt and freshly ground pepper to taste

IN A LARGE BOWL, combine beans, tuna, celery, tomatoes, and parsley. In a small bowl, whisk all dressing ingredients together. Toss with bean mixture. Taste and adjust seasoning.

CURRIED LENTIL AND RICE SALAD

In an earthy tumble of rice and lentils, the juicy acid-sweetness of dried apricots plays against the smoky taste of roasted peppers. For the latter, a good imported brand is the best choice unless you're in the mood to roast the peppers yourself (see page 32). And if you're really ambitious, you can substitute fresh papaya for the apricots.

1 cup lentils

1 cup long-grain white rice

2 roasted red peppers, cut into strips

4 scallions, thinly sliced

6 dried apricots, soaked in hot water for 30 minutes, drained, and cut into strips

1 cup fresh cilantro leaves, coarsely chopped

DRESSING:

2 tablespoons fresh lemon juice

2 tablespoons balsamic vinegar

1 teaspoon honey

1 1/2 teaspoons curry powder

1/2 teaspoon ground cumin

1/4 cup olive oil

Salt and freshly ground pepper to taste

COOK LENTILS in salted simmering water until tender, about 25 minutes. Drain and let cool. **COOK RICE,** covered, in salted simmering water for 18 minutes. Let cool. **IN A LARGE BOWL,** combine lentils, rice, peppers, scallions, apricots, and half of cilantro. In a small bowl, whisk all dressing ingredients together. Toss with lentil mixture. Add salt and pepper. Garnish with remaining cilantro.

LIMA BEAN, PROSCIUTTO, AND PARMESAN SALAD

Prosciutto and Parmesan give this salad a certain Italian sensibility, and the splash of sherry vinegar adds Iberian flair. The best sherry vinegars are from Spain, but the dish can taste dramatically different depending on which one you choose. Like wine collectors, sherry vinegar enthusiasts have several kinds in the pantry.

One 10-ounce package frozen lima beans, cooked
    and cooled
8 cherry tomatoes, quartered
3 thin slices prosciutto, cut into julienne
2 cups baby spinach leaves, coarsely chopped
$^{1}/_{2}$ cup grated Parmigiano-Reggiano cheese
3 tablespoons olive oil
2 tablespoons sherry vinegar
1 teaspoon dried oregano
Salt and freshly ground pepper to taste

IN A LARGE BOWL, combine beans, tomatoes, prosciutto, spinach, and cheese. In a small bowl, whisk oil, vinegar, and oregano together. Toss with bean mixture. Add salt and pepper.

SOUTHWESTERN PASTA SALAD

Only a few years ago, salsa seemed exotic and daring. The basic idea, a zesty mix of raw ingredients used as a topping, fired the imagination of even the most traditionally trained chefs. Salsas quickly became part of the widespread interest in ethnic ingredients and highly spiced condiments. Proof that this was no passing fancy came in 1991, with the astonishing news that salsa sales had surpassed sales of ketchup! This easily made salad captures the bright, rich flavors of the Southwest in a salsa-tossed tangle of spaghetti, sausage, and vegetables.

1 pound spaghetti, broken into 4-inch lengths

2 cups fresh corn kernels (about 4 ears)

SALSA DRESSING:

1/2 cup salsa verde

3 tablespoons olive oil

3 tablespoons fresh lime juice

Pinch of sugar

2 small zucchini, diced

4 Roma (plum) tomatoes, seeded and diced

1 roasted red bell pepper, roasted, peeled, and cut into strips (see page 32)

8 ounces smoked fully cooked andouille or other spicy sausage, thinly sliced

Salt and freshly ground pepper to taste

1/2 cup fresh cilantro leaves, coarsely chopped

COOK SPAGHETTI according to package directions. Drain and let cool. **COOK CORN** in salted boiling water for 3 minutes. Drain and let cool. **IN A SMALL BOWL,** stir all dressing ingredients together. In a large bowl, combine spaghetti, corn, zucchini, tomatoes, bell pepper, and sausage. Toss with dressing. Add salt and pepper. Sprinkle with cilantro.

COOL AS A CUCUMBER SESAME NOODLES

This Asian-inspired salad is so versatile you can make it, or a reasonable facsimile, at a moment's notice. Warm, nutty flavors contrast with the coolness of mint and cucumber. A few cups of leftover meat quickly transforms this dish into a main course.

DRESSING:

2 tablespoons smooth peanut butter

2¹/₂ tablespoons Asian sesame oil

2¹/₂ tablespoons low-salt soy sauce

¹/₄ cup water

2 cloves garlic, minced

1 tablespoon minced fresh ginger

1 tablespoon honey

¹/₄ teaspoon red pepper flakes

1 pound rice noodles or spaghetti

1 English (hothouse) cucumber, peeled, halved lengthwise, seeded, and thinly sliced

4 scallions, thinly sliced

¹/₄ cup fresh mint leaves, coarsely chopped

¹/₄ cup fresh cilantro leaves, coarsely chopped

2 cups cooked poultry, shrimp, or meat, diced (optional)

COOK NOODLES according to package directions. Drain and let cool. In a small bowl, whisk all dressing ingredients together until smooth. In a large bowl, combine noodles with remaining ingredients. Toss with dressing and serve at room temperature or chill before serving.

WILD RICE AND RED LENTIL SALAD

The plane was late, the fridge empty, stomachs were growling, no one wanted to go to the store. It was one of those nights when, meal-wise, things could have gone horribly wrong. But somehow the available ingredients, humble though they may seem alone, came together as if someone had planned this hearty little salad deliberately. It has something for everyone: the crunch of pepper and celery; the tang of citrus; a toothsome mix of olives, lentils, and rice. It's a real gem, and it's definitely for one of those nights . . .

DRESSING:

6 tablespoons sherry vinegar

2 tablespoons fresh orange juice

2 tablespoons fresh lemon juice

2 anchovy fillets, mashed

1 small shallot, minced

1/2 cup olive oil

2 cups wild rice

1 cup red lentils

1 red bell pepper, seeded, deribbed, and cut into strips

2 celery stalks, thinly sliced

1 cup imported black olives, pitted and halved

1/2 cup green olives, pitted and halved

1/2 red onion, diced

1/2 cup chopped fresh parsley

1 cup walnuts, toasted and coarsely chopped (see page 32)

Salt and freshly ground pepper to taste

COOK WILD rice, covered, in salted simmering water until firm-tender, about 35 minutes. Drain and let cool. Cook lentils in salted simmering water for 10 minutes. Drain and let cool. In a small bowl, whisk all dressing ingredients together until smooth. In a large bowl, combine wild rice, lentils, and all remaining ingredients. Taste and adjust seasoning.

RISI E BISI SALAD

Veneto is Italy's northeastern most region, stretching from the sea deep into the mountains. It has a varied climate and an equally diverse cuisine, but its culinary pride is risi bisi, a mixture of rice and the spectacularly sweet peas of the region. Purists once insisted that, for complete legitimacy, the peas must be grown between the towns of Chiogga and Burano. The dish sounds simple enough, but it is not without controversy. It's a vegetable dish, say some; no, it's a soup, contend others. Although our version seems decidedly unsouplike, we know better than to enter this Venetian fray. Let's just say that for our risi e bisi, you need a fork.

1 cup Arborio rice

2 cups fresh or frozen peas

$^1/_2$ cup imported black olives, halved and pitted

1 small red onion, chopped

$^1/_2$ cup chopped fresh parsley

4 ounces diced prosciutto, country ham, or leftover
   cooked chicken

DRESSING:

$^1/_4$ cup chopped fresh parsley

1 clove garlic, minced

$^1/_4$ cup chicken stock

2 tablespoons olive oil

2 tablespoons fresh lemon juice

Salt and freshly ground pepper to taste

COOK RICE in 2 cups salted simmering water until water is absorbed, about 20 minutes. Fluff and let cool. Cook peas in salted boiling water for 3 minutes. Drain and let cool. **IN A LARGE BOWL,** combine rice, peas, olives, onion, parsley, and ham or chicken. In a small bowl, whisk all dressing ingredients together. Toss with rice mixture. Taste and adjust seasoning.

BLACK-EYED PEA, TURKEY, AND SUN-DRIED TOMATO SALAD

Call it the era of the olive, this fortunate time we live in that has rediscovered the wonders of the olive in all its forms. The most humble neighborhood deli often offers an array of olives; the oil of the olive is touted both for its taste and health properties; and olive-based breads, sauces, and spreads abound. Of the latter, tapenade is the classic, a versatile mixture of anchovies, capers, and olives spiced with everything from garlic and herbs to Cognac and rum. Sometimes called Provençal caviar, it is available everywhere and is the secret ingredient in this readily made pantry favorite.

DRESSING:

2 tablespoons olive tapenade

3 tablespoons balsamic vinegar

2 tablespoons olive oil

4 cups cooked black-eyed peas, drained and rinsed

2 zucchini, shredded

8 oil-packed sun-dried tomatoes, drained and cut
  into strips

2 cups diced cooked turkey

3 cups baby spinach leaves, torn into bite-sized
  pieces

Salt and freshly ground pepper to taste

IN A SMALL BOWL, whisk all dressing ingredients together. In a large bowl, combine remaining ingredients. Toss with dressing. Add salt and pepper.

The exact equivalents in the following tables have been rounded for convenience.

LIQUID / DRY MEASURES

U.S.	Metric
¼ teaspoon	1.25 milliliters
½ teaspoon	2.5 milliliters
1 teaspoon	5 milliliters
1 tablespoon (3 teaspoons)	15 milliliters
1 fluid ounce (2 tablespoons)	30 milliliters
¼ cup	60 milliliters
⅓ cup	80 milliliters
½ cup	120 milliliters
1 cup	240 milliliters
1 pint (2 cups)	480 milliliters
1 quart (4 cups, 32 ounces)	960 milliliters
1 gallon (4 quarts)	3.84 liters
1 ounce (by weight)	28 grams
1 pound	454 grams
2.2 pounds	1 kilogram

OVEN TEMPERATURE

Fahrenheit	Celsius	Gas
250	120	½
275	140	1
300	150	2
325	160	3
350	180	4
375	190	5
400	200	6
425	220	7
450	230	8
475	240	9
500	260	10

LENGTH

U.S.	Metric
⅛ inch	3 millimeters
¼ inch	6 millimeters
½ inch	12 millimeters
1 inch	2.5 centimeters